LEASING COMMERCIAL PREMISES

by

MARK PAWLOWSKI
LLB (Hons), BCL (Oxon.), ACIArb., Barrister,
Professor of Property Law, School of Law, *University of Greenwich*

2004

A division of Reed Business Information
ESTATES GAZETTE
151 WARDOUR STREET, LONDON W1F 8BN

First published in 1999 by Chandos Publishing (Oxford) Limited
This reformatted edition published by Estates Gazette in September 2002

Reprinted 2004

ISBN 0 7282 0390 1

© M. Pawlowski, 1999

Printed in Great Britain

For my late father, Kazimierz,
who gave me an education

Contents

Preface. ix
The Author xiii
Table of Cases xv
Table of Statutes xxiii

1	**Nature of a Lease** 1
	1.1 Freehold and leasehold estates. 1
	1.2 The essentials of a valid lease. 2
	1.3 Formalities of a lease. 9
	1.4 Types of leases and tenancies 10

2	**Rent, Insurance and Service Charges**. 15
	2.1 Rent. 15
	2.2 Insurance 23
	2.3 Service charges. 26

3	**Disrepair** 29
	3.1 Introduction 29
	3.2 General principles of construction. 29
	3.3 Decorative repairs 32
	3.4 The extent of the demised premises. 32
	3.5 Repair contrasted with improvement 33
	3.6 Notice of the disrepair. 35
	3.7 Implied obligations to repair 36
	3.8 Liability in tort. 37
	3.9 Remedies for breach of a repairing obligation 38

4	**Assignment and Subletting**. 45
	4.1 Introduction 45
	4.2 When can the tenant assign, sublet? 45
	4.3 What amounts to unreasonable withholding of consent? 46
	4.4 Authorised guarantee agreements. 58
	4.5 What acts by the tenant constitute a breach? 59

4.6   Landlord's remedies for breach 60
4.7   Tenant's remedies where consent unreasonably
       withheld. 60

5   Other Covenants 63
5.1   Introduction 63
5.2   Quiet enjoyment. 63
5.3   Non-derogation from grant. 67
5.4   Alterations and improvements. 68
5.5   User. 71
5.6   Options to renew / purchase 72

6   Enforceability of Covenants 75
6.1   Introduction 75
6.2   Liability of the original tenant 75
6.3   Liability of the original landlord 81
6.4   Liability of an assignee 82
6.5   Liability of a surety 84
6.6   Disclaimer of leases. 86
6.7   Liability of and to a stranger to the lease 88
6.8   The Contracts (Rights of Third Parties) Bill. 89

7   Termination of Leases 91
7.1   Introduction 91
7.2   Forfeiture 91
7.3   Surrender of the lease 101
7.4   Expiry of time. 103
7.5   Notice to quit 103
7.6   Abandonment of premises 104
7.7   Disclaimer of the lease. 105
7.8   Exercise of an express power in the lease 105
7.9   Frustration 107
7.10   Acceptance of a repudiatory breach. 108
7.11   Parties' rights on termination 110

8   Statutory Protection 113
8.1   Introduction 113
8.2   Application of Part II. 114
8.3   Automatic continuance and non-statutory
       methods of termination. 116
8.4   Statutory machinery for termination / renewal 117
8.5   Terms of the new tenancy. 126

8.6   Tenant's claim to compensation for disturbance
       and improvements.............................. 128
8.7   Landlord's application for interim rent 130

Appendix 1   Oyez specimen Lease of Shop Premises 133
Appendix 2   British Property Federation Short-term
              Commercial Lease........................ 139

Preface

My aim in writing this book is to provide the reader with a concise outline of the law relating to commercial lettings. I have attempted to cover the most salient areas, but unavoidably it has been necessary to omit certain topics in order to comply with publishing and cost constraints. The book, therefore, gives no more than a broad insight into the area and is not intended to be an exhaustive study of the subject.

My brief has been to write a book on commercial leases which does not exceed 50,000 words in length. This has been no easy task, particularly with the recent upsurge of case law and statutory intervention in the landlord and tenant field. That said, it is hoped that the book will provide a useful summary of the relevant law for those requiring a general knowledge of the key principles affecting commercial lettings. It is envisaged that it will also provide a useful text for both law (and non-law) students embarking on a landlord and tenant course at graduate and post-graduate level. In particular, I have in mind surveying and estate management students who often find some of the 'weightier tomes' on landlord and tenant somewhat overwhelming.

Two major changes in landlord and tenant law have dominated the scene in the last decade. The first involves the loss of privity of contract after 1 January 1996. The Landlord and Tenant (Covenants) Act 1995 has fundamentally altered the enforcement of leasehold covenants producing a complex 'duality' of rules on enforceability; the new legislation does not have retrospective effect and leases granted before 1 January 1996 continue to be enforced under the pre-Act law. The subject is dealt with in Chapter 6.

The second major legislative change has been the Landlord and Tenant Act 1988, which was aimed to redress the imbalance in the strength of the landlord's control over the process of alienation of leases. The Act reverses the burden of proof and makes it incumbent on the landlord to show that a refusal of consent to an assignment of the lease, subletting, etc, was reasonable in all the circumstances, backed by the sanction of damages if the landlord fails in his statutory duties. The subject of unreasonable refusal of consent to an assignment or subletting continues to be of real practical importance to both landlords and tenants of commercial leases. It is discussed fully in Chapter 4.

There is no doubt that the law of landlord and tenant, particularly in relation to commercial lettings, is complex and obscure. The commercial lease itself is invariably a lengthy and unintelligible document. There are no common form clauses (dealing with repairs, insurance, rent review, service charges, etc) which are universally adopted by the legal profession. The forfeiture clause, which entitles the landlord to end the lease upon the tenant's default, is an excellent example of the law's complexity in the field of landlord and tenant. The writer's work on the subject, entitled *The Forfeiture of Leases*, (Sweet & Maxwell, 1993) runs into 400 pages and contains no less than 500 cases, some of which date back to the seventeenth century! In 1985, the Law Commission, as part of its programme for the codification of leasehold law, published a Report entitled *Forfeiture of Tenancies* (1985, Law Com. No. 42) which examined various defects in the current law and recommended the entire replacement of the present structure with an entirely new system. Over 14 years have passed since the publication of this Report but there is still little expectation that the Law Commission's recommendations will become law in the near future. In the meantime, there have been interesting judicial developments seeking to extend purely contractual doctrines into the leasehold context, in particular, the doctrine of repudiatory breach, which is discussed in Chapter 7 together with other methods of termination of a lease.

Business tenancies are governed by Part II of the Landlord and Tenant Act 1954, which provides statutory protection to tenants of commercial premises. There is a vast body of case law which has emerged over the years interpreting the various provisions of Part II. The Act and relevant case law is considered in Chapter 8.

This Preface would be incomplete without an expression of my warmest thanks to my wife, Lidia, who has once again had to endure my absences from home in order to research and write this latest text on leasehold law. Thankfully, I have managed to complete the manuscript somewhat ahead of schedule so as to leave time for summer holidays and 'quality time' with friends and family before the start of the next academic session. I would also like to thank my colleagues at the School of Law, who have enabled me to pursue my legal writing by undertaking various teaching and administrative responsibilities which I would otherwise have had to bear on my own. I also wish to thank my publishers, Chandos Publishing (Oxford) Ltd, for commissioning this work and for their diligent efforts in bringing my manuscript to print. A debt of gratitude is also owed to Sweet & Maxwell Ltd for kindly allowing me to reproduce the British Property Federation's recently published Short-Term Commercial Lease in Appendix 1. I also wish to thank the Solicitor's Law Stationery Society Limited for their kind permission to reproduce their specimen lease of shop premises for illustrative purposes only. The law is stated to be as at 1 August 1999.

Mark Pawlowski
School of Law
University of Greenwich
August 1999

The Author

Mark Pawlowski is a Barrister and Professor of Property Law at the School of Law, University of Greenwich. He is also a Visiting Lecturer in Property Law at University College London.

He has written extensively on a variety of land law and landlord and tenant subjects and is the author of a number of books including *The Forfeiture of Leases* (Sweet & Maxwell, 1993) and the *Doctrine of Proprietary Estoppel* (Sweet & Maxwell, 1996). He is also co-author of *A Casebook on Rent Review and Lease Renewal* (with Diana Brahams) (1986, BSP Ltd), *Casebook on Landlord and Tenant Law* (with James Brown) (Sweet & Maxwell, 1995) and *Law Q. & A.: Landlord and Tenant* (with James Brown) (Blackstone Press, 1995).

He is the Editor of *Rent Review and Lease Renewal* (LLP Ltd) and General Editor of *Landlord and Tenant Review* (Sweet & Maxwell).

He read law at Warwick University and Wadham College, Oxford. He practised at the Chancery Bar for 11 years and currently holds a door tenancy at Pepys' Chambers, 17 Fleet Street, Strand, London. He has been a full-time academic since 1983. Apart from teaching at undergraduate and postgraduate levels, he also lectures to the legal and surveying professions. His primary academic interests lie in the fields of land law, landlord and tenant, and equity and trusts.

Married to Lidia de Barbaro, Mark lives in Kenilworth, Warwickshire. His main recreations include foreign travel, tennis and the movies. He and Lidia have been to most places in the world including the Amazon jungle, the Andes, Nepal, China, the Maldives, Hawaii, South Africa, Canada, the United States, the Arctic Circle and the Antarctic.

The author may be contacted at the following address:

The School of Law
University of Greenwich
Mansion Site
Avery Hill Campus
London SE9 2PQ

Telephone: 020 8331 9040
Fax: 020 8331-8473
e-mail: m.pawlowski@gre.ac.uk

Table of Cases

A Plesser & Co Ltd v *Davis* (1983) 267 EG 103. 85

Adagio Properties Ltd v *Ansari* [1998] 35 EG 86 94

Adami v *Lincoln Grange Management Ltd*, The Times, December
22, 1997 37

Air India v *Balabel* [1993] EG 90 47

Allnatt London Properties Ltd v *Newton* [1984] 1 All ER 423. 46

Ashburn Anstalt v *Arnold* [1989] Ch 1 6

Associated British Ports v *CH Bailey plc* [1990] 2 AC 703. 40

Associated Dairies Ltd v *Pierce* (1983) 265 EG 127 84

Bacchiocchi v *Academic Agency Ltd* [1998] 2 All ER 241. 129

Bagettes Ltd v *GP Estates Ltd* [1956] Ch 290. 7

Baker v *Merckel* [1960] 1 QB 657. 77

Bandar Property Holdings Ltd v *JS Darwen (Succesors) Ltd* [1968] 2 All
ER 305 23

Barclays Bank plc v *Daejan Investments (Grove Hall) Ltd* [1995] 18
EG 117 72

Barrett v *Lounova (1982) Ltd* [1990] 1 QB 348 37

Bassairi Ltd v *Camden London Borough Council* [1998] EGCS 27. 7

Bates v *Donaldson* [1896] 2 QB 241. 55

Baxter v *Camden London Borough Council (No 2)* [1999] 1 All ER 237 64

Beacon Carpets Ltd v *Kirby* [1984] 3 WLR 489 24

Bell v *General Accident Fire & Life Assurance Corporation Ltd* [1997]
EGCS 174. 13

Berrycroft Management Co Ltd v *Sinclair Gardens Investments
(Kensington) Ltd* [1997] 1 EGLR 27

Bickel v *Duke of Westminster* [1977] QB 517. 49

Billson v *Residential Apartments Ltd* [1992] 1 All ER 141. 100

Bishop v *Consolidated London Properties Ltd* (1933) 102 LJKB 257. 36

Booker v *Palmer* [1942] 2 All ER 674. 8

Boyer v *Warbey* [1953] 1 QB 234. 82

Branchett v *Beaney* [1992] 3 All ER 910 64

Breams Property Investment Co Ltd v *Stroulger* [1948] 2 KB 1 5

Bretherton v *Paton* [1986] 1 EGLR 172 8

Bristol Cars Ltd v *RKH (Hotels) Ltd* (1979) 38 P & CR 411 122

British Bakeries (Midlands) Ltd v *Michael Testler & Co Ltd* [1986] 1
EGLR 64 55,56

British Telecommunications plc v *Sun Life Assurance Society plc* [1995]
  4 All ER 44. 35
Bromley Park Garden Estates Ltd v *Moss*[1982] 1 WLR 1019 49
Brown v *Gould* [1972] Ch 53. 73
Browne v *Flower* [1911] 1 Ch 219 67
Bush Transport Ltd v *Nelson* [1987] 1 EGLR 71 102

Caerphilly Concrete Products Ltd v *Owen* [1972] 1 WLR 372 11
Campden Hill Towers v *Gardner* [1977] QB 823 31
Carradine Properties Ltd v *Aslam* [1976] 1 All ER 573. . . . . 103, 119
Celsteel Ltd v *Alton House Holdings Ltd (No 2)* [1987] 2 All ER 290 83
Centaploy Ltd v *Matlodge Ltd* [1974] Ch 1 5
Central Estates (Belgravia) Ltd v *Woolgar (No 2)* [1972] 1 QB 48 96
Central London Property Trust Ltd v *High Trees House Ltd* [1947]
  KB 130 . . . . 17, 19
Chartered Trust plc v *Davies* [1997] 2 EGLR 83. 108
Chatsworth Estates Ltd v *Fewell* [1931] 1 Ch 224 89
Cheshire Lines Committee v *Lewis & Co* (1880) 50 LJQB 121 5
City of London Corporation v *Fell* [1993] 2 All ER 449 76
City & Metropolitan Properties Ltd v *Greycroft Ltd* (1987) 283 EG 199 81
Cohen v *Tanner* [1900] 2 QB 609. 65
Collins v *Flynn* [1963] 2 All ER 1068 30
Comber v *Fleet Electrics Ltd* [1955] 2 All ER 161 72
Co-operative Insurance Society Ltd v *Argyll Stores (Holdings) Ltd* [1997]
  3 All ER 297. 41
Re Cooper's Lease (1968) 19 P & CR 541 54
Connaught Restaurants Ltd v *Indoor Leisure Ltd* [1993] 46 EG 184 43
Re Cosh's Contract [1897] 1 Ch 9. 58
Cottage Holiday Associates Ltd v *Customs and Excise Commissioners*
  [1983] QB 735 2
Crago v *Julian* [1992] 1 WLR 372 10
Crane v *Morris* [1965] 1 WLR 1104. 114
Crayford v *Newton* (1886) 36 WN 54 32
Credit Suisse v *Beegas Nominees Ltd* [1994] 4 All ER 803. 30
Creska Ltd v *Hammersmith and Fulham London Borough Council*
  [1998] 37 EG 165 35

Dellneed Ltd v *Chin* (1987) 53 P & CR 172. 8
Department of the Environment v *Allied Freehold Property Trust*
  [1992] 45 EG 156 131
Dinefwr Borough Council v *Jones* (1987) 284 EG 58 36
Dolgellau Golf Club v *Hett* [1998] 34 EG 87 125
Dong Bang Minerva (UK) Ltd v *Davina Ltd* [1995] 5 EG 162. . . . . . 48, 54, 57
Drane v *Evangelou* [1978] 1 WLR 455. 63
Duke of Westminster v *Guild* [1985] QB 688 . . . . 37, 38

Duke of Westminster v *Swinton* [1948] 1 KB 524 68
Duncliffe v *Caerfelin Properties Ltd* [1989] 27 EG 89. 83

Eastern Telegraph Co Ltd v *Dent* [1899] 1 QB 835. 60
Electricity Supply Nominees Ltd v *IAF Group Ltd* [1993] 1 WLR 1059. 43
Electricity Supply Nominees Ltd v *National Magazine Co Ltd*
   [1998] EGCS 162 42
Elite Investments Ltd v *TI Bainbridge Silencers Ltd* (1986) 280 EG 1001 . . . 33
Elliston v *Reacher* [1908] 2 Ch 374 89
Escalus Properties Ltd v *Robinson* [1995] 3 WLR 524 28
Esselte AB v *Pearl Assurance plc* [1997] 1 WLR 891 117
Esso Petroleum Co Ltd v *Fumegrange Ltd* (1994) 68 P & CR D15. 9
Estates Gazette Ltd v *Benjamin Restaurants Ltd* (1994) 26 EG 140. 82
Expert Clothing Service & Sales Ltd v *Hillgate House Ltd* [1986] Ch 340. . . 95

FW Woolworth and Co Ltd v *Lambert* [1937] Ch 37 69
FW Woolworth plc v *Charlwood Alliance Properties Ltd* (1986) 282
   EG 585 55
Farimani v *Gates* (1984) 271 EG 887. 96
Farr v *Ginnings* (1928) 44 TLR 249. 53
Finchbourne Ltd v *Rodrigues* [1976] 3 All ER 581. 27
Footwear Corporation Ltd v *Amplight Properties Ltd* [1998] 3 All ER 52 . . . 48
Fox v *Jolly* [1916] AC 1 94
Friends' Provident Life Office v *British Railways Board* [1996] 1 All
   ER 336 78

Gardner & Co v *Cone* [1928] Ch 955. 72
Garston v *Scottish Widows' Fund and Life Assurance Society* [1998]
   3 All ER 596. 106
Goldstein v *Saunders* [1915] 1 Ch 549. 53
Re 14 Grafton Street, London W1 [1971] Ch 935 119
Graysim Holdings Ltd v *P & O Property Holdings Ltd* [1996] 1
   AC 329 . . . . 6, 115
Greater London Council v *Connolly* [1970] 2 QB 100 15
Re Greater London Properties Ltd's Lease [1959] 1 WLR 503. . . . . 54, 57
Gregson v *Cyril Lord Ltd* [1963] 1 WLR 41. 125
Griffin v *Pillet* [1926] 1 KB 17. 36
Guppy's (Bridport) Ltd v *Brookling* (1984) 269 EG 846. 63
GUS Management Ltd v *Texas Homecare Ltd* [1993] 27 EG 130 78

Hafton Properties Ltd v *Camp* [1993] EGCS 101. 64
Hagee (London) Ltd v *AB Erikson and Larson* [1976] QB 209 . . . . 12, 115
Haines v *Florensa* [1990] 09 EG 70 70
Hall v *Howard* [1988] 44 EG 83. 36
Halsall v *Brizell* [1957] Ch 169 89

Harding v *Preece* (1882) 9 QBD 281 88
Harmer v *Jumbil (Nigeria) Tin Areas Ltd* [1921] 1 Ch 200 67
Hart v *Emelkirk Ltd* [1983] 1 WLR 1289. 44
Havenridge Ltd v *Boston Dyers Ltd* [1994] 49 EG 111. 23
Hemingway Securities Ltd v *Dunraven Ltd* [1995] 09 EG 322. 60
Herbert Duncan Ltd v *Cluttons* [1993] 2 All ER 449. 76
Hill v *East and West India Dock Co* [1884] 9 App Cas 448. 87
Hillil Property & Investment Co Ltd v *Naraine Pharmacy Ltd* (1979)
    252 EG 1013. 114
Hindcastle Ltd v *Barbara Attenborough Associates Ltd* [1996] 1 All
    ER 737 86
Holme v *Brunskill* (1878) 3 QBD 495 85
Hughes v *Waite* [1957] 1 All ER 603 58
Hussein v *Mehlman* [1992] 32 EG 59. .... 42, 108

Ingram v *Inland Revenue Commissioners* [1997] 4 All ER 395 3
International Drilling Fluids Ltd v *Louisville Investments (Uxbridge)*
    Ltd [1986] Ch 513 50

Jenkin R Lewis & Son Ltd v *Kerman* [1971] Ch 477. 102
Jenkins v *Jackson* (1888) 40 Ch 71 65
Jervis v *Harris* [1996] Ch 195 41
Jeune v *Queen's Cross Properties Ltd* [1974] Ch 97 42
John Lewis Properties plc v *Viscount Chelsea* [1993] 34 EG 116. .... 97, 108
Johnsey Estates Ltd v *Webb* [1990] 19 EG 84. 85
Junction Estates Ltd v *Cope* (1974) 27 P & CR 482 85

Kammins Ballrooms Co Ltd v *Zenith Investments (Torquay) Ltd*
    [1971] AC 850 123
Kellog MW Ltd v *F Tobin*, unreported, 8 April 1999 79
Kelly v *Battershell* [1949] 2 All ER 830 67
Kelly v *Rodgers* [1892] 1 QB 910. 65
Kenny v *Preen* [1963] 1 QB 499. 64
Killick v *Second Covent Garden Property Co* [1973] 1 WLR 658. 54
Re King, (Deceased) Robinson v *Gray* [1963] Ch 459. .... 24, 76, 81
King's Motors (Oxford) Ltd v *Lax* [1969] 3 All ER 665 73
Kleinwort Benson Ltd v *Lincoln City Council* [1998] 3 WLR 1095 18
Kumar v *Dunning* [1987] 3 WLR 1167 85

Lace v *Chantler* [1944] KB 368. 4
Lambert v *FW Woolworth & Co Ltd* [1938] Ch 883. 69
Lee v *K Carter Ltd* [1949] 1 KB 85. 54
Lee-Verhulst (Investments) Ltd v *Harwood Trust* [1973] 1 QB 204. ..... 7, 115
Leeds v *Cheetham* (1827) 1 Sim 146. 25
Lemmerbell Ltd v *Britannia LAS Direct Ltd* [1998] 48 EG 188 106

Linden v *Department of Health and Social Security* [1986] 1 WLR 164......7
Liverpool City Council v *Irwin* [1977] AC 239......37
Liverpool Properties Ltd v *Oldbridge Investments Ltd* (1985) 276 EG 1352 94
London & Associated Investment Trust plc v *Calow* (1986) 280 EG 1252 8
Lurcott v *Wakeley* [1911] 1 KB 905 34

Malzy v *Eicholz* [1916] 2 KB 308......66
Manfield & Sons Ltd v *Botchin* [1970] 2 QB 612......12
Mannai Investment Co Ltd v *Eagle Star Life Assurance Co Ltd* [1997] AC 749......106
Matthew v *Curling* [1922] 2 AC 180 17
McAuley v *Bristol City Council* [1992] 1 All ER 749 38
Meadows v *Clerical, Medical and General Life Assurance Society* [1981] Ch 70......91
Middlegate Properties Ltd v *Bilbao, Caroline Construction Co Ltd* (1972) 24 P & CR 329 83
Midland Bank plc v *Chart Enterprises Inc* [1990] 44 EG 68......47
Re *Midland Railway Co's Agreement* [1971] Ch 725 5
Miller v *Emcer Products Ltd* [1956] Ch 304......64
Milmo v *Carreras* [1946] KB 306......3
Re *Mirror Group (Holdings) Ltd*, The Times, 12 November 1992 77
Morcom v *Campbell-Johnson* [1956] 1 QB 106......34
Moss Bros Group plc v *CSC Properties Ltd* [1999] EGCS 47......55
Moule v *Garrett* (1872) LR 7 Ex 101 ......77, 81
Mullaney v *Maybourne Grange (Croydon) Management Co Ltd* [1986] 1 EGLR 70 26
Mumford Hotels Ltd v *Wheler* [1964] Ch 177 24
Murphy v *Sawyer-Hoare* [1993] 27 EG 127......88

National Carriers Ltd v *Panalpina (Northern) Ltd* [1981] AC 675......17, 25, 107
National Grid Co plc v *M25 Group Ltd* [1999] 08 EG 169......21
Next v *National Farmers'Union Mutual Insurance Co* [1997] EGCS 181...46
Norfolk Capital Group Ltd v *Kitway Ltd* [1977] QB 506 49
Norris v *Checksfield* [1991] 1 WLR 1241......8
Norwich Union Life Insurance v *Low Profile Fashions* (1992) 64 P & CR 187 77
Norwich Union Life Insurance Society v *Shopmoor Ltd* [1998] 3 All ER 32 52
Nurdin & Peacock plc v *DB Ramsden & Co Ltd (No 2)* [1999] 1 All ER 941 18
Nynehead Developments Ltd v *RH Fibreboard Containers Ltd* [1999] 02 EG 139......43, 109

Oliver Ashworth (Holdings) Ltd v *Ballard (Kent) Ltd* [1999] 2 All
    ER 791 110
O'Brien v *Robinson* [1973] AC 912 36
Orlando Investments Ltd v *Grosvenor Estate Belgravia* (1989) 59
    P & CR 21 53
Owen v *Gadd* [1956] 2 QB 99 64

P & ASwift Investments v *Combined English Stores Group plc* [1988]
    3 WLR 313 . . . . 76, 85
Parker v *Boggon* [1947] KB 346. 49
Perera v *Vandiyar* [1953] 1 WLR 672 64
Perry v *Chotzner* (1893) 9 TLR 488. 32
Pierson v *Harvey* (1885) 1 TLR 430. 97
Pimms Ltd v *Tallow Chandlers Co* [1964] 2 QB 547. 55
Ponderosa International Development Inc v *Pengap Securities (Bristol)*
    Ltd [1986] 1 EGLR 66 51
Poppets (Caterers) Ltd v *Maidenhead Corporation* [1971] 1 WLR 69. 124
Port v *Griffith* [1938] 1 All ER 295 67
Post Office v *Aquarius Properties Ltd* [1987] 1 All ER 1055 34
Premier Confectionery (London) Co Ltd v *London Commercial Sale*
    Rooms Ltd [1933] Ch 904. 56
Premier Rinks v *Amalgamated Cinematograph Theatres Ltd* (1912) 56
    SJ 536 52
Preston Borough Council v *Fairclough* (1982) 8 HLR 70 102
Proudfoot v *Hart* (1890) 25 QBD 42. . . . . 30, 32
Prudential Assurance Co Ltd v *London Residuary Body* [1992] 2 AC 386. . . . 4
Prudential Assurance Co Ltd v *Mount Eden Land Ltd* [1997] 1 EGLR 37. . . 46

Queensway Marketing Ltd v *Associated Restaurants Ltd* (1988) 32
    EG 41 66

R v *Paulson* [1921] 1 AC 271. 96
Rainbow Estates Ltd v *Tokenhold Ltd* [1998] 3 WLR 980. . . . . 40, 42
Ravenseft Properties Ltd v *Davstone (Holdings) Ltd* [1980] QB 12 . . . . . 33, 35
Reynolds v *Phoenix Assurance Co Ltd* (1978) 247 EG 995. 25
Richmond v *Savill* [1926] 2 KB 530 102
Rimmer v *Liverpool City Council* [1985] QB 1. 37
Robinson v *Kilvert* (1889) 41 Ch 88. 67
Rolph v *Crouch* (1867) LR 3 Ex 44. 110
Romulus Trading Co Ltd v *Comet Properties Ltd* [1996] 2 EGLR 70 68
Rye v *Rye* [1962] AC 496. 3

Sanderson v *The Mayor of Berwick-on-Tweed Corporation* [1884] 13
    QBD 547. 66
Savva v *Hussein* (1997) 73 P & CR 150. 95

Scala House & District Property Co Ltd v *Forbes* [1974] 1 QB 575 95
SEDAC Investments Ltd v *Tanner* [1982] 1 WLR 1342. 41
Segal Securities Ltd v *Thoseby* [1963] 1 QB 887. 96
Selous Street Properties Ltd v *Oronel Fabrics Ltd* (1984) 270 EG 643 . . . 77, 85
Sharp v *McArthur and Sharp* [1987] 19 HLR 364. 8
Sheldon v *West Bromwich Corporation* (1973) 25 P & CR 360 36
Shell-Mex and BP Ltd v *Manchester Garages Ltd* [1971] 1 WLR 612 8
Skipton Building Society v *Clayton* (1993) 66 P & CR 223 10
Smallwood v *Sheppards* [1895] 2 QB 627. 2
Smedley v *Chumley & Hawke Ltd* (1981) 261 EG 775. 31
Smith v *Northside Developments Ltd* (1987) 283 EG 1211. 8
Sobey v *Sainsbury* [1913] 2 Ch 513 89
Southwark London Borough Council v *Mills* [1998] 2 EGLR 30 64
Spencer's Case (1583) 5 Co Rep 16a 82
Sportoffer Ltd v *Erewash Borough Council* [1999] EGCS 37 56
Stacey v *Hill* [1901] 1 QB 660 86
Star Rider Ltd v *Inntrepreneur Pub Co* [1998] 16 EG 140 43
Stening v *Abrahams* [1931] 1 Ch 470. 59
Straudley Investments Ltd v *Mount Eden Land Ltd* [1997] EGCS 175 53
Street v *Mountford* [1985] AC 809. . . . . 6, 114
Sudbrook Trading Estate Ltd v *Eggleton* [1983] 1 AC 44 74
Swanson v *Forton* (1949) Ch 143. 54

Thomas Bookman Ltd v *Nathan* [1955] 1 WLR 815. 54
Re Thompson and Cottrell's Contract [1943] Ch 97 87
Re Town Investments Ltd Underlease [1954] Ch 301 49
Tredegar (Viscount) v *Harwood* [1929] AC 72 24
Tulk v *Moxhay* (1848) 2 Ph 774. 88

United Scientific Holdings Ltd v *Burnley Borough Council* [1978]
 AC 904. 20
Universities Superannuation Scheme Ltd v *Marks & Spencer plc* [1999]
 04 EG 158. 18

Vaux Group plc v *Lilley* [1991] 04 EG 136. 57
Venetian Glass Gallery Ltd v *Next Properties Ltd* [1989] 2 EGLR 42. 57
Venus Investments Ltd v *Stocktop Ltd* (1997) 74 P& CR D23 9

WH Smith Ltd v *Wyndham Investments Ltd* [1994] EGCS 94. 87
Wallace v *Manchester City Council* [1998] 41 EG 223. 42
Walsh v *Lonsdale* (1882) 21 Ch D9 10
Warnford Investments Ltd v *Duckworth* [1979] Ch 127. 87
Warren v *Keen* [1954] 1 QB 15. 38
Warren v *Marketing Exchange for Africa Ltd* [1988] 2 EGLR 247. 56
West Country Cleaners (Falmouth) Ltd v *Saly* [1966] 3 All ER 210. 73

Wettern Electric Ltd v *Welsh Development Agency* [1983] QB 796 37
Williams v *Earle* (1868) LR 3 QB 739 60
William Hill (Southern) Ltd v *Waller* [1991] 1 EGLR 271. 85
Willmott v *London Road Car Co Ltd* [1910] 2 Ch 525 54
Windmill Investments (London) Ltd v *Milano Restaurants Ltd* [1962]
    2 QB 373. 96
Wolfe v *Hogan* [1949] 2 KB 194. 96

Young v *Ashley Gardens Properties Ltd* [1903] 2 Ch 112. 53
Youngmin v *Heath* [1974] 1 All ER 461. 17

Zenith Investments (Torquay) Ltd v *Kammins Ballrooms Co Ltd (No 2)*
    [1971] 1 WLR 1751 122

Table of Statutes

Arbitration Act 1996. 20
  s60 21
  s68(1) 21
  s68(2) 21
  s69(1) 20
  s69(3) 21
  s69(8) 21

Common Law Procedure Act 1852
  s210. . . . . 16, 94, 98
  s212 98
Contracts (Rights of Third Parties) Bill. 89
County Courts Act 1984
  s138(2) 98
  s138(4) 99
  s138(9A). 99
  s138(10) 100
  s139 94
  s139(1) 16
  s139(2) 99
  s139(3) 99
Criminal Law Act 1977
  s6 . . . . 93, 104

Defective Premises Act 1972
  s4(1) 37
  s4(4) 37
Deserted Tenements Act 1817 104
Distress for Rent Act 1689 23
Distress for Rent Act 1737
  s16 104
  s18. 110

Explosives Act 1875 67

Fires Prevention (Metropolis) Act 1774
s83 25

Housing Act 1985
  s610. . . . . 70, 72
Housing Act 1988
  s27(3) 66

Insolvency Act 1986
  ss172–182. 105
  s178 105
  s178(4) 86, 87
  s178(6) 86
  ss306–317. 105
  s315 86

Landlord and Tenant Act 1730
  s1 110
Landlord and Tenant Act 1927
  Part I 71
  s1(1) 130
  s3 . . . . 78, 121
  s9 71
  s18(1) 38, 39
  s18(2) 104
  s19 58
  s19(1) 46, 47, 50, 57
  s19(1)(a). 57
  s19(2) 68
  s19(3) 72
  s19(4) 72
Landlord and Tenant Act 1954
  Part II 2, 6, 9, 12, 13, 54, 72, 76, 85, 109, 113, 114
  Part III 129
  s23. 114
  s23(1). 9, 114, 115
  s23(2) 114
  s23(3) 123
  s24(1). 76, 116, 119
  s24(3)(a) 117
  ss24–28. 116
  s24(2) 91, 103
  s24A 130, 131
  s25. 113, 118, 119, 121, 122, 123, 126, 128
  s26 . . . . 113, 118, 120, 122, 123, 126, 128
  s27 121
  s27(1). 116, 117
  s27(2). 116, 117

s28. 117
s29 126
s30. 117
s30(1) 119
s30(1)(a)–(g). 121, 123
s30(1)(a) 123
s30(1)(b). 123
s30(1)(c) 124
s30(1)(d). 124
s30(1)(e) 124
s30(1)(f) 124, 126
s30(1)(g). 125
s30(2) 126
s30(3) 125
s31A 125, 126
s31(2) 126
s32(2) 126
s33. . . . . 120, 127
s34. . . . . 127, 131
s35 128
s37(1) 128
s37(3) 128
s38 129
s38(1) 46
s38(4) 116
s38(4)(a) 114
s40. 118
s40(2) 118
s40(3) 118
s42(3) 125
s43. . . . . 114, 115
s43(3) 115
s47 130
s52 89
s53 61
s54 105
s64. . . . . 122, 130
s64(1) 127
Landlord and Tenant Act 1985
s8 36
s11. . . . . 31, 36, 42
Landlord and Tenant Act 1988. . . . . 45, 46
s1 46
s1(3) 46, 37, 61
s1(4) 47

s1(6) 47, 48, 52
s2 47
s3 47
s4 61
Landlord and Tenant (Covenants) Act 1995. . . . . 22, 58, 77
s2 79
s4 93
s17. . . . . 78, 81, 85
s18 78
s19 88
Land Registration Act 1925
s24 81
s24(1) 77
Law of Distress Amendment Act 1888 23
Law of Property Act 1922
Schedule 15 11
Law of Property Act 1925
s1 1
s44 89
s52(1) 9, 102
s52(2)(c) 102
s53(1)(a). 102
s54(2) 9
s72(4) 3
s77 81
s77(1)(c) 77
s78 88
s79(1) 75
s84. . . . . 70, 72, 89
s139 102
s141(1) 76
s142(1) 83
s144 57
s146 39
s146(1) 75, 94, 104
s146(2) 40, 100
s146(3) 101
s146(4) 99
s146(10) 101
s147. . . . . 32, 40
s149(3) 5
s149(6) 10
s196 104
s205(1)(ix) 3
Law of Property Act 1969. . . . . 125, 130

Law of Property (Miscellaneous Provisions) Act 1989
  s2(1) 10
Leasehold Property (Repairs) Act 1938. . . . . 40, 41, 95
Limitation Act 1980
  s15 12

Metropolitan Police Courts Act 1839
  s13 105

Occupiers' Liability Act 1957. 38

Protection from Eviction Act 1977
  s1 66
  s2 93

Race Relations Act 1976
  s24 45
  s24(2) 52
Recorded Delivery Service Act 1962. 121
  s1 104
Rentcharges Act 1977
  s2 15

Sex Discrimination Act 1975
  s31 45
  s31(2) 52
Sexual Offences Act 1956
  s35(2) 92
Stamp Act 1891
  s14 10
Supreme Court Act 1981
  s37 44

Town and Country Planning Act 1990 1

Unfair Contract Terms Act 1977 43

Chapter 1

Nature of a Lease

1.1 Freehold and leasehold estates

An estate in land may be defined as a certain legal status for a period of time. The concept of an estate is, therefore, to do with time – for how long land is held. By virtue of s1 of the Law of Property Act 1925, only two estates in land are capable of subsisting or of being created or conveyed in law, namely, a 'fee simple absolute in possession' (commonly known as a freehold estate) and a 'term of years absolute' (commonly referred to as a leasehold estate).

The 'fee simple' is the greatest estate known to English land law. The word 'fee' means that it is an estate capable of inheritance and 'simple' signifies that it is inheritable by heirs generally. Thus, a fee simple estate will end only if there ceases to be any heirs of X (X being the current owner) who dies without disposing of the estate under his will. If this happens, the land will revert to the Crown as *bona vacantia* since, under the doctrine of tenures, all land in England and Wales ultimately belongs to the Crown (or the Duchy of Lancaster or Cornwall, as appropriate).

The holder of a freehold estate is entitled to unrestricted use and enjoyment of the land, subject to (a) any third party rights created over the land (eg an easement of a right of way over the land or a restrictive covenant); (b) statutory restrictions and duties (eg under the Town and Country Planning Act 1990); and (c) the general law of negligence, nuisance and trespass. A freeholder also enjoys various rights of alienation in respect of the land; in other words, he is entitled to lease, mortgage, gift and sell it, if he so wishes.

A term of years absolute is also a legal estate but it is less enduring than a fee simple because it is for a definite period of time. The term may be just for one year, a fraction of a year, or a number of years. A lease may also be periodic, which may be weekly, monthly, quarterly or yearly. It is evident that a lease may be granted for any duration, no matter how short or long. It has even been suggested that a lease may endure for a few days or even hours. At the other end of the spectrum, it is possible for a term of

years to be granted for very long periods of time (ie many hundreds or thousands of years). The longest lease on record is an Irish lease comprising a grant, on 3 December 1868, for a term of *10 million years* in respect of a plot for a sewerage tank! It is, of course, also possible to grant a lease comprising an aggregate of discontinuous periods of time: see *Smallwood* v *Sheppards* (1895), where it was recognised that a right of occupation for three successive bank holidays could constitute a single letting, and *Cottage Holiday Associates Ltd* v *Customs and Excise Commissioners* (1983), where a right to occupy a holiday cottage for one week in each year for a term of 80 years was upheld as a valid lease for 80 weeks.

The leaseholder's rights and obligations are determined by the general law but, more importantly, by the terms of the lease itself. Thus, the tenant will usually covenant to pay the rent, repair the premises, use the property only for the purposes designated by the lease, and not assign, sublet, charge or part with possession of the land without the landlord's consent. Essentially, there are two types of lease: (a) fixed term; and (b) periodic (see 1.2.4). A fixed term will come to an end by expiry of time (when the term expires). A periodic tenancy will end upon the expiration of a notice to quit served by either the landlord or the tenant on the other party.

This book focuses on the leasing of commercial premises, but much of the general law of landlord and tenant is applicable to both business and residential premises. Apart from the basic common law principles, there is also a vast body of highly complex statutory provisions which govern most forms of letting. In the commercial context, business tenants are afforded a large measure of security of tenure under Part II of the Landlord and Tenant Act 1954: see, Ch. 8. Anyone embarking on a study of commercial landlord and tenant law must, therefore, acquire an understanding not only of the basic common law principles but also the statutory regime governing the letting of business premises.

1.2 The essentials of a valid lease

A lease will generally arise where an estate owner (the landlord) grants to another (the tenant) the right to exclusively possess land for an ascertainable period, while himself retaining a reversionary interest, being either a freehold, or a leasehold of longer duration than that demised to the tenant. There are a number of essential prerequisites to the creation of a valid lease (whether commercial or residential). These are considered below.

1.2.1 Parties to a lease

The landlord and tenant, respectively, must be different persons. In other words, a landlord cannot grant a lease of land to himself. This proposition may be illustrated by the case of *Rye* v *Rye* (1962), where two brothers, who were in partnership together as solicitors, purported to grant a lease of the office premises (which they owned as freeholders) to themselves. The House of Lords held that it was not legally possible for a person to grant himself a lease of land of which he was also the owner. The rationale is that a lease creates a division of ownership between landlord and tenant. If the landlord and tenant are one and the same person, there is a merger of freehold and leasehold estates and no division of ownership occurs. For this reason, a nominee cannot grant a lease to his principal since he cannot contract with his principal so as to create rights and obligations in relation to the subject of the nomineeship: *Ingram* v *Inland Revenue Commissioners* (1997). However, a statutory exception allows Ato grant a lease to Aand B. Similarly, Aand B can grant a lease to A(or B): see s72(4) of the Law of Property Act 1925.

1.2.2 Subject-matter must be land

The subject-matter of the lease must be land. Land has an extended meaning for this purpose and includes not just the ground itself but any buildings on the land, as well as 'incorporeal hereditaments' (rights over land): see s205(1)(ix) of the Law of Property Act 1925. It is, therefore, possible to have a lease of fishing rights, or mining rights. Livestock and chattels cannot form the subject-matter of a lease, but they may be hired out under a hiring agreement governed by the law of contract and bailment.

1.2.3 Grant must be of a lesser estate

If a tenant divests himself of everything he owns (ie his leasehold estate), which he must do if he transfers to his subtenant an estate as great as his own, the relationship of landlord and tenant cannot exist between him and the so-called subtenant. In effect, in this situation, the tenant will have *assigned* (ie transferred) all his interest in the property. The point arose in *Milmo* v *Carreras* (1946), where the plaintiff was the tenant of a flat under a lease for a term of seven years expiring on 28 November 1944. On 25 October 1943, he agreed to sublet the flat to the defendant for one year from 1

November 1943, and thereafter quarterly until either party should give three months' notice to quit. Because of the quarterly extension, the subterm would necessarily extend beyond the expiration of the headlease. The Court of Appeal held that the plaintiff had, by virtue of the agreement, transferred to the defendant the *whole* of the term existing under the headlease and he retained no reversion. Accordingly, he had no right to possession of the premises.

1.2.4 *Certainty of term*

The term or duration of the lease must be certain. Thus, a tenancy 'for the duration of the war' has been held invalid as being for an uncertain term: *Lace* v *Chantler* (1944). The doctrine of certainty of term applies to both fixed and periodic tenancies. In regard to the former, the maximum duration of the term must be ascertainable at the outset of the lease. This does not usually give rise to any difficulties since the lease will expressly set out the duration and commencement date of the term (eg 'to hold unto the tenant from the 1st day of January 1999 for the term of 10 years').

In relation to a periodic tenancy, however, it may be said that the ultimate length of the tenancy cannot be determined at the outset – it could go on forever and is dependent on either party serving a notice to quit. But, so long as each separate period is definite (ie a week, month, quarter or year), the test of certainty of duration is satisfied. In *Prudential Assurance Co Ltd* v *London Residuary Body* (1992), Lord Templeman explained:

> A tenancy from year to year is saved from being uncertain because each party has power by notice to determine at the end of any year. The term continues until determined as if both parties made a new agreement at the end of each year for a new term for the ensuing year.

Closely related to the rule regarding certainty of term is the doctrine of repugnancy. The basic proposition here is that a clause *totally* precluding a party from determining a periodic tenancy is repugnant to the nature of such a tenancy and of no effect. In the *Prudential Assurance* case, the lease provided that 'the tenancy shall continue until the land is required by the [landlord] for the purpose of widening the highway'. The House of Lords held that the lease was void (because it was for an uncertain period) and that the land was held on a yearly tenancy created by virtue of the tenant's possession and payment of a yearly rent. Moreover, since the clause preventing the landlord from determining the tenancy until the land was required for road-widening purposes was inconsistent with the right of either party under a yearly tenancy to terminate it by notice to quit, it was ineffective to preclude the landlord from serving such a notice bringing the tenancy to an end.

Another leading case is *Centaploy Ltd* v *Matlodge Ltd* (1974), where an agreement to let a garage contained the following words: 'Received the sum of £12, being one week's rent . . . and to continue until determined by the lessee'. The Court held that the document provided for a weekly tenancy and, although the term making the tenancy determinable only by the lessee did not make the periodic tenancy thus created void for uncertainty, nevertheless, a term whereby a landlord could never have the right to terminate a periodic tenancy was repugnant to the nature of such a tenancy and void. The practical significance of this finding was that, despite the terms of the agreement, the landlord was free to serve a notice to quit on the tenant bringing the weekly tenancy to an end: see also *Cheshire Lines Committee* v *Lewis & Co* (1880).

A *partial* fetter, however, on the right to serve a notice to quit will not be considered repugnant to the grant of a periodic tenancy. Thus, in *Re Midland Railway Co's Agreement* (1971), it was suggested by Russell LJ that a curb for 10, 20 or 50 years should not be rejected as repugnant to the concept of a periodic tenancy. In *Breams Property Investment Co Ltd* v *Stroulger* (1948), various agreements for quarterly tenancies contained a clause that the landlords would not, during the period of three years from the beginning of the tenancies, serve notice to quit on the tenants except in the event of the landlords requiring the premises for their own occupation and use. The Court of Appeal held that, as the clause merely attached a condition to the quarterly right to give notice (by suspending it during the first three years of the tenancies except in the event of the landlords requiring possession for their own use), it was not repugnant to the nature of a quarterly tenancy. In effect, the doctrine of repugnancy was side-stepped by construing the lease in a particular way.

1.2.5 Reversionary leases

A term which is expressed to commence more than 21 years from the date of the lease creating it is void under s149(3) of the Law of Property Act 1925. Subject to this qualification, a landlord may wish to grant a reversionary lease whose term is expressed to commence at some date after its execution (not being more than 21 years). For example, the premises may be subject to an existing lease which is not due to expire until some specified date in the future.

1.2.6 Distinction between leases and licences

A tenancy creates an estate in land. A licence, on the other hand, is a mere permission to occupy land which, without that permission, would constitute a trespass. A licence, therefore, creates no proprietary interest in land binding on third parties: *Ashburn Anstalt* v *Arnold* (1989).

The lease must grant the tenant exclusive possession of the demised premises. The test whether an occupancy of commercial (or residential) premises is a tenancy or a licence is whether, on the true construction of the agreement, the occupier has been granted exclusive possession of the premises for a fixed or periodic term at a stated rent: *Street* v *Mountford* (1985), involving residential accommodation. If the property is granted for a term at a rent with exclusive possession, the grant falls to be characterised as a tenancy regardless of the parties' intentions and the labels which the parties may have put on the written document in so far as this may not accord with the surrounding circumstances including, in particular, the nature and extent of the occupation. Indeed, in this situation, any express reservation to the landlord of *limited* rights to enter and view the state of the premises, and to repair and maintain the property, only serve to emphasise the fact that the occupier is entitled to exclusive possession and is a tenant. It has, however, been suggested since *Street* that the reservation of a rent is not strictly necessary for the creation of a tenancy: *Ashburn Anstalt* v *Arnold* (1989). There may, however, be special circumstances which negate the presumption of a tenancy:

- *Where the occupier is a 'lodger'* in the sense that the landlord provides attendance or services which require the landlord (or his employees or agents) to exercise unrestricted access to and use of the premises. Although the term 'lodger' is more apposite in the context of residential accommodation, it may also be of considerable relevance in the commercial context. A tenant who carries on the business of subletting residential accommodation at the demised premises will normally fall outside the statutory protection conferred on business tenants under Part II of the Landlord and Tenant Act 1954: see Ch 12. In *Graysim Holdings Ltd* v *P & O Property Holdings Ltd* (1996), the House of Lords ruled that intermediate landlords who are not themselves in actual physical occupation of the premises are not protected under Part II because the 1954 Act makes no provision for dual occupation of premises (ie a business tenant and his subtenant cannot enjoy statutory protection under Part II in respect of the same premises). The House of Lords, however, did not rule out the possibility that, in exceptional cases, the rights reserved by the tenant might be so extensive that he would remain in occupation of the property for the purposes of Part II. The crux of the matter lies in the distinction between two earlier authorities (discussed in *Graysim*), namely *Bagettes Ltd* v *GP Estates Ltd* (1956) and *Lee-Verhulst (Investments) Ltd* v *Harwood Trust* (1973). In the former, the residential flats were let unfurnished and, although the tenant provided hot water for the subtenants and cleaned the common parts, the 'service' element was negligible: see also *Bassairi Ltd* v *Camden London Borough Council* (1998). By contrast, in the *Verhulst* case, the lettings comprised furnished rooms with substantial services (ie supply of bedlinen, daily cleaning of rooms and regular change of linen, and provision of light meals if required). The Court of Appeal held that, in view of the degree of control and extent of the services provided, the tenant 'occupied' the entire premises for the purpose of its business, namely that of 'providing furnished accommodation and services for those residing there'. In *Graysim* itself, it was suggested that, where the letting takes the form of a subtenancy, the subtenant will be entitled to exclusive possession of the sublet part and, hence, will be the 'occupier' to the exclusion of the tenant. At the other end of the spectrum, however, where the occupancy takes the form of a *licence*, there will often be more room for argument that the tenant retains occupation of the property because the rights granted by a licence will be less extensive than those comprised in a subtenancy. The key elements in the *Verhulst* case were the provision of services to the occupants (who were characterised as licensees) and the unrestricted entry to each room necessary to perform those services: see also *Linden* v *Department of Health and Social Security* (1986), involving eight self-contained flats managed by a district health authority. By contrast, in *Graysim*, neither the tenant nor his agents had any right of access to the units, nor did they have keys or means of access. All the occupants had exclusive possession and each was a subtenant in respect of his unit;

• *Where, from the outset, there is no intention to create legal relations*. This is more applicable in the residential context. For example in *Booker* v *Palmer* (1942), the owner of a cottage agreed to allow a friend to install an evacuee in the cottage rent-free for the duration of the war. The Court of Appeal held that there was no intention on the part of the owner to enter into legal relationships with the evacuee. If, on the other hand, the parties are commercial people contracting at arm's length, there is a strong presumption that the parties intend to enter into a legally binding relationship, unless there is a clear statement to the contrary;

- *Where possession is granted pursuant to a contract of employment.* An employee of the landlord will be a licensee if he is genuinely required to occupy his employer's premises for the better performance of his duties: *Norris* v *Checksfield* (1991). In these circumstances, the possession of the employee is treated as the possession of the employer and the relationship of landlord and tenant is not created;

- *Where the relationship between the parties is that of vendor and purchaser.* In most cases, the contract of sale of the land will expressly stipulate that, if the purchaser enters into occupation prior to completion of the purchase, his status will be that of a mere licensee (and not tenant): see *Sharp* v *McArthur and Sharp* (1987) and *Bretherton* v *Paton* (1986).

Prior to the *Street* decision, the question whether an agreement gave rise to a tenancy or licence depended on the intention of the parties to be derived from the whole of the document in question. This approach was applied in several cases, all dealing with the lease/licence distinction in the context of business occupation. In *Street*, Lord Templeman, in his review of the authorities, referred to the case of *Shell-Mex and BP Ltd* v *Manchester Garages Ltd* (1971), involving the occupancy of a commercial garage, emphasising that the agreement there could only be regarded as a licence if it did not confer the right of exclusive possession, and that no other test for distinguishing between a tenancy and a licence appeared workable. In *Dellneed Ltd* v *Chin* (1987), the Court applied the test put forward in Street to a commercial letting involving the operation of a Chinese restaurant. Similarly, in *London & Associated Investment Trust plc* v *Calow* (1986) the Court applied the *Street* principle to a letting of premises comprising solicitors' offices. Again, in *Smith* v *Northside Developments Ltd* (1987), the *Street* test was applied to an oral agreement to share shop space in a market.

It is apparent from all these cases that the question as to whether or not exclusive possession has been conferred on a business occupier is a matter to be derived not only from the written agreement itself but also its surrounding factual matrix. More recently, in *Esso Petroleum Co Ltd* v *Fumegrange Ltd* (1994), the Court of Appeal applied the *Street* principle in relation to the occupation of two service stations. In this case, the licence agreement referred to the owner's 'right of possession and control of the service station' and required the occupier not to impede in any way the exercise of that right. These rights were held to be quite inconsistent with an exclusive right to possession of the stations. In particular, the degree of physical control by the owner was very significant and quite genuine. In *Venus Investments Ltd* v *Stocktop Ltd* (1997), a case involving garage premises, the Court expressly held that the test enunciated by the House of Lords in *Street* applied equally to commercial property. In this case, the licence agreement contained no reference to possession or exclusive possession. The Court concluded that, in the case of commercial property rather than residential property, no inference of exclusive possession could be made. Moreover, unlike most commercial leases, no provision was reserved in the agreement to the landlord for entry or inspection of the premises and there was no right of re-entry (ie forfeiture clause) for breach. It was also clear from the parties' correspondence that they had intended to create only a licence agreement.

The most important practical effect of categorising the occupier as a licensee (as opposed to a tenant) is that he will have no statutory protection under Part II of the Landlord and Tenant Act 1954: see Ch 8. Section 23(1) of the 1954 Act talks in terms of a 'tenancy' and, therefore, by implication licences are excluded from the operation of Part II.

1.3 Formalities of a lease

Section 52(1) of the Law of Property Act 1925 provides that all conveyances of land (or of any interest therein) are void for the purpose of conveying or creating a legal estate unless made by deed. A lease is a conveyance for this purpose and, hence, the general rule is that a lease must be made by deed to be legally valid.

One important exception to this rule is contained in s54(2) of the 1925 Act, which provides that no writing is required for a lease taking effect in possession (ie the tenant is entitled to immediate occupation) for a term not exceeding three years (which includes all periodic tenancies) at a full economic rent. In other words, such a lease will be a valid legal lease despite the absence of writing. A void lease at law (ie not complying with the legal formality of a deed under s52(1)) may still take effect as a contract for a lease which equity may enforce by means of a decree of specific performance under the rule in *Walsh v Lonsdale* (1882). Moreover, if the tenant goes into possession under a void lease at law and pays rent by reference to a weekly period, a weekly tenancy will be presumed from the fact that the agreed rental is referable to a weekly period. The weekly tenancy will then take effect as a legal lease under the exception contained in s54(2).

Where the parties enter into a *contract* for the grant of a lease in the future, such contract must be made in writing in order to comply with s2(1) of the Law of Property (Miscellaneous Provisions) Act 1989.

If the tenant wishes to assign his tenancy, he must use a deed. The requirement of a deed applies to the assignment of any tenancy, even a weekly tenancy, which was created orally pursuant to s54(2) (see above): *Crago v Julian* (1992).

Most formal leases must be duly stamped in order to be admissible in evidence in civil proceedings: s14 of the Stamp Act 1891.

1.4 Types of leases and tenancies

Leases (or tenancies) are categorised as being either specific (fixed term) or periodic. With fixed term tenancies, the duration of the tenancy is fixed for a definite period starting from the commencement date of the term. Periodic tenancies, on the other hand, simply continue from period to period until determined at the end of any given period by a notice to quit served by either party on the other. It is common for periodic tenancies to run on a weekly, monthly, quarterly or yearly basis. It is fundamental to the operation of any periodic tenancy that either party has the ability to serve a notice to quit terminating the tenancy. Thus, any provision which completely fetters this right is void (see above).

Fixed term tenancies may take a number of different forms:

- *Tenancy determinable with a life*. It is possible to create a tenancy which is expressed to determine automatically with the dropping of the life of the tenant or landlord, or some other person. By virtue of s149(6) of the Law of Property Act 1925, such a lease is converted into one for a fixed period of 90 years, if it is granted at a rent. In *Skipton Building Society v Clayton* (1993), it was held that the occupiers of a flat who, in return for some money, had been granted a licence to occupy the flat rent-free for the rest of their lives had, in reality, been given a lease and not a licence and that the lease was caught by s149(6) and duly converted into a 90-year term on the basis that the words 'at a rent or in consideration of a fine' in the subsection included the payment of a premium, which was held to have been paid on the facts;

- *Concurrent lease (or lease of the reversion)*. This arises where the landlord grants a lease to T1 and subsequently grants a lease to T2 of the same premises for a term to commence before the expiry of the lease in favour of T1. So long as the leases are concurrent, the disposition in favour of T2 operates as a part assignment of the landlord's reversion entitling T2 to the rent reserved in T1's lease and the benefit of the covenants given by T1. If T1's lease is prematurely determined before T2's lease has expired, T2 will be entitled to possession of the premises. However, forfeiture (see Ch 7) by the landlord of T2's lease cannot affect T1, for although T1's lease is akin to a subtenancy, it is not derived out of T2's lease. Often such leases are created so as to give a lender security for his loan in relation to the premises;

- *Perpetually renewable lease*. If a lease contains an option to renew in favour of the tenant under which the new lease is to include the option to renew, a perpetually renewable lease will exist and, in accordance with Schedule 15 to the Law of Property Act 1922, will be converted into a 2000 year term determinable by the tenant by 10 days' notice expiring on any date upon which the original lease would have expired if it had not been renewed: *Caerphilly Concrete Products Ltd v Owen* (1972). From the landlord's standpoint, the consequences of a perpetually renewable lease are very severe. With perpetually renewable leases, the original rent payable becomes the rent of the 2000 year term. The question whether a particular form of words confers a right to perpetual renewal is one of construction, and such a right will only be upheld where there exist plain and unambiguous words. Not suprisingly, the courts are reluctant to hold that a lease contains the seeds of its own infinite reproduction.

Apart from fixed and periodic tenancies, there are also a number of other types of tenancy. These are listed below:

- *Tenancy at will*. A tenancy at will exists where land is occupied 'at the will' of the landlord (ie with the consent of the landlord). However, because the permitted occupation is for an uncertain period, it is not a 'term of years absolute' and, hence, may be determined by the landlord at any time by a demand for possession. If possession is demanded, the tenant must leave immediately. Such tenancies may arise expressly (where the parties expressly create such a tenancy), or by operation of law (from the conduct of the parties where, for example, a tenant holds over rent free at the end of the lease with the landlord's permission). In *Manfield & Sons Ltd* v *Botchin* (1970), the landlords of business premises agreed to let a shop to the tenant until such time as they succeeded in getting permission to develop the site. A written tenancy agreement stated that the tenancy was to be a tenancy at will, that the tenant should pay an annual rent on the landlord's demand, and that Part II of the Landlord and Tenant Act 1954 (affording statutory protection to business tenants) should not apply. The Court held that the tenancy agreement operated to create a tenancy at will (and not a yearly tenancy). The case establishes that a tenancy at will created by express agreement does not fall within the scope of Part II of the 1954 Act. The decision was followed and applied in *Hagee (London) Ltd* v *AB Erikson and Larson* (1976), where the Court of Appeal held that a tenancy at will, whether created by operation of law or by express agreement, was outside Part II. The courts, however, will be astute to detect sham tenancies at will which do not reflect the true intentions of the parties. In *Hagee*, the Court of Appeal emphasised that it would look 'behind the label' in order to determine whether a tenancy at will was a genuine reflection of the parties' intentions;

- **Tenancy at sufferance.** This denotes the relationship of owner and occupier where the tenant holds over on the expiry of his lease and the landlord has neither consented nor expressed objection. The legal effects of this relationship will depend on subsequent events. Thus, if the landlord requires the tenant to quit, the tenant becomes a trespasser. If, on the other hand, the landlord signifies his consent (eg by a demand for rent), the tenant becomes a tenant at will and, if rent is paid with reference to a particular period, the tenant becomes a periodic tenant. Alternatively, if the landlord simply acquiesces, he will be statute barred from reclaiming possession if he fails to re-assert his title within 12 years from the date that the tenant's possession ceased to be lawful: s15 of the Limitation Act 1980;

- **Tenancy by estoppel.** The doctrine of estoppel precludes parties, who have induced others to rely upon their representations, from denying the truth of the facts represented. For the purpose of landlord and tenant law, this means that neither the landlord nor the tenant can question the validity of the lease granted, once possession has been taken up. Thus, even if the landlord is not the true owner of the estate out of which the tenant is granted his lease, the tenant cannot deny any of his leasehold obligations to the landlord by arguing that the grant was not effectively made. Similarly, the landlord cannot set up his want of title as a ground for repudiating the lease. The estoppel tenancy does not, however, bind the true owner (ie the person claiming under title paramount) unless there is evidence that he has accepted the tenancy. If the tenant is actually turned out by the true owner during the currency of the lease, he can claim damages for the eviction against the landlord if there is an express covenant for quiet enjoyment covering interruption by title paramount.

If the landlord subsequently acquires the legal estate out of which the tenancy could have been created (eg by purchasing the freehold), this 'feeds the estoppel' and makes it good in interest. If this happens, the tenant acquires a legal tenancy founded upon the landlord's newly acquired legal estate. A tenancy by estoppel of business premises comes within the statutory protection afforded to business tenants under Part II of the Landlord and Tenant Act 1954: *Bell v General Accident Fire & Life Assurance Corporation Ltd* (1997).

Chapter 2

Rent, Insurance and Service Charges

2.1 Rent

Rent is a profit issuing out of and derived from the demised land payable by the tenant to the landlord as consideration for the possession of the land during a given term. It is essentially a payment which the tenant is bound by his contract to make to his landlord for the use of land.

It is usual for a lease to contain a formal 'reddendum' containing words such as 'yielding and paying' or 'paying therefor' which fixes the amount of rent payable. This is followed by an express covenant by the tenant to pay the rent reserved. A reservation of rent is not, however, a vital prerequisite for the existence of a tenancy and, in the absence of a rent covenant in the lease, one will automatically be implied by operation of law. Rent falls to be distinguished from other periodical payments:

- *Rentcharges*. These are charged on the land in perpetuity (or for a term of years) with an express power of distress (see 2.1.6), but the owner of the rentcharge has no reversion on the land charged (ie he is not a landlord). By s2 of the Rentcharges Act 1977, rentcharges cannot generally be created after 22 August 1977;
- *Premiums*. These are capital sums payable as a lump sum (or in instalments) from the commencement of the term;
- *Payments for insurance*. Although at common law, these are not rent, the lease will usually expressly reserve them as part of the rent (so as to enable a distress to be levied for unpaid premiums);
- *Service charges*. These are payments representing a proportion of the landlord's costs incurred in repairing, maintaining and insuring the premises. They will usually be expressly recoverable as rent so that they may, in default, be destrained for by the landlord.

2.1.1 Certainty of rent

The rent payable by the tenant must be calculable with certainty at such time as when payment becomes due. In *Greater London Council* v *Connolly* (1970), the rent books of numerous council tenants provided that the weekly rent was 'liable to be increased or decreased on notice being given' by the landlord. The Court of Appeal held that, although the amount of any increased rent was dependent on the act of the landlord, it could be calculated with certainty at the time when payment became due and so was not uncertain. The rent would be fixed when the landlord served the required notice and, hence, certain by the time it became payable.

A rent calculated by reference to the index of retail prices is sufficiently certain, as is a sum representing say, 10 per cent of the turnover of the tenant's business.

2.1.2 *Formal demand for rent*

If the tenant fails to pay the rent as required by the lease, the landlord may sue the tenant for any arrears owing. The action for rent arrears is a debt action for a liquidated sum and one founded in contract (ie the tenant will be in breach of his covenant to pay rent). In addition to claiming the arrears, the landlord may seek to forfeit the lease for non-payment of rent: see further, Ch 7, at 7.2.

At common law, the landlord can only forfeit for non-payment of rent if he has made a formal demand for the rent. The demand must be made by the landlord or his agent at the demised premises (or other place of payment agreed) on the last day of payment at such convenient hour before sunset in order that adequate time can be given to the tenant to raise the money required. The demand must be for the last instalment only. This precondition can be (and in practice always is) dispensed with by reserving a right of re-entry (ie forfeiture) for non-payment of rent 'whether formally demanded or not'. By statute, a formal demand is also unnecessary where at least six months' rent is in arrears and no sufficient distress is to be found on the demised premises countervailing the arrears then due: s210 of the Common Law Procedure Act 1852. In the County Court, the relevant provision is contained in s139(1) of the County Courts Act 1984.

2.1.3 *Obligation to pay rent*

In the absence of contrary provision, rent will be payable in arrears. However, the lease will invariably provide for the rent to be paid 'in advance'. In the case of fixed term and yearly tenancies, the rent is expressed to be payable on the usual quarter days (ie 25 March

(Lady Day), 24 June (Midsummer Day), 29 September (Michaelmas Day), and 25 December (Christmas Day). Rent is due on the morning of the day specified for payment, but it is not in arrears until midnight. If the rent day falls on a Bank Holiday, it is not due until the following day.

Payment of the rent must be made by the tenant to the landlord (or their duly authorised agents). Payment by a stranger does not absolve the tenant of his obligation unless the payment is authorised by him or subsequently ratified. The rent must be paid in lawful currency and the reservation 'yielding and paying' (see 2.1) implies payment in cash. A landlord can, therefore, refuse to accept payments of rent by cheque, unless by prior agreement. If a cheque is accepted, payment is conditional upon it being honoured. The landlord is entitled to the rent in full, less any deductions specifically authorised by the lease or statute. For example, the lease may provide that the rent is to be paid 'without any deduction or set-off whatsoever'. This will preclude the tenant from deducting the cost of any repairs incurred by him from current or future rent.

Although the tenant is under a strict obligation to pay rent throughout the term, it may be possible to absolve himself from liability in certain circumstances. First, a tenant may claim that his obligation to pay rent is suspended where he is evicted by title paramount. Thus, if a third party evicts the tenant claiming to do so by a lawful title superior to that of the landlord, the obligation to pay rent is suspended entirely during the period of eviction: *Matthew* v *Curling* (1922). Secondly, the tenant may argue that the landlord is estopped (precluded) from claiming the rent arrears if he has represented to the tenant that he will not seek to recover them and the tenant, on the faith of that representation, alters his position so that he is no longer able to pay them: see *Central London Property Trust Ltd* v *High Trees House Ltd* (1947). Thirdly, the landlord's claim may be time-barred by virtue of s19 of the Limitation Act 1980 (ie the landlord's claim for rent arrears may be issued outside the requisite six year time limit). Fourthly, the tenant may contend that his liability for rent arrears ceased (or was suspended) on the occurrence of a frustrating event discharging the lease: see *National Carriers Ltd* v *Panalpina (Northern) Ltd* (1981), Ch 7, at 7.9. The lease will usually contain a clause suspending the tenant's liability to pay rent pending reinstatement of the demised premises following a fire.

The obligation to pay rent, however, under a periodic tenancy continues until the tenancy has been determined by a valid notice to quit: *Youngmin* v *Heath* (1974).

2.1.4 *Overpayment or underpayment of rent/service charges*

The House of Lords has recently ruled that money paid under a mistake of law can be recovered by the payer even where payment had been made under a settled understanding of the law at the time or where payment had been received by the payee under an honest belief of an entitlement to retain the money: *Kleinwort Benson Ltd* v *Lincoln City Council* (1998). The case has huge potential consequences in respect of overpayments of rent, service charges and other periodical payments payable under a lease.

In *Nurdin & Peacock plc* v *DB Ramsden & Co Ltd (No 2)* (1999), the Court held that various overpayments of rent under a commercial lease were paid under a mistake of law and hence, under the *Kleinwort* principle, recoverable by the payer. Similarly, in *Universities Superannuation Scheme Ltd* v *Marks & Spencer plc* (1999), a tenant was obliged to make up underpayments of service charges in respect of its store, despite the fact that they resulted from an error in calculating the service charge on the landlord's part. The service charge certificate (which had been issued by the landlord) was not stated in the lease to be final and conclusive and, accordingly, was open to challenge by both the landlord and tenant.

2.1.5 *Rent review*

As well as containing an express covenant to pay rent, the lease will invariably include a rent review clause allowing for the revision of the initial rent either upwards or downwards (or both). The purpose of such a clause is usually to provide the landlord with a safeguard against the effects of inflation and thus to ensure that he receives from the tenant a rent which reflects the market value of the demised premises at any given time.

If the lease reserves the *same* rent throughout the term, the courts will not imply a rent review clause as business efficacy does not require it (ie the lease is workable without such a clause). In such circumstances, the tenant is only liable to pay the initial level of rent reserved under the lease. However, during the currency of the lease, the parties may enter into an agreement whereby the tenant agrees to pay the landlord a higher rent in return for some consideration on the landlord's part, for example, the funding of alterations or improvements to the property. Such an agreement runs collateral to the lease itself and is binding on the parties. If the landlord unilaterally reduces the rent, he may be estopped from reneging on the reduction where the tenant has relied and acted upon the landlord's promise, even though the tenant gave no consideration for the rent reduction: *Central London Property Trust Ltd* v *High Trees House Ltd* (1947), referred to above at 2.1.3.

Unfortunately, there exists no commonly accepted standardised form of rent review clause. (But see the *Law Society/RICS Model Forms of Rent Review Clause* (1985 Edition)). However, certain elements are common to most rent review clauses. Such a clause will, for example, invariably specify the periods or intervals as to when the rent should be reviewed, and also a formula by which the new rent will be calculated. A common formula is based on that rent which a hypothetical willing tenant would pay for the premises to a hypothetical willing landlord as at the date of review. If any matters are to be assumed in relation to the determination of the new rent (eg the length of the term, vacant possession, compliance with tenant's covenants, user of premises, etc) or to be disregarded (eg rent-free occupation by the tenant, tenant's improvements during the term, the effect of a tenant's or subtenant's occupation, etc), these will be expressly set out in the review clause. Otherwise, if the clause is silent or unclear, the terms of the 'hypothetical lease' after a rent review will be assumed to be the same as those of the actual lease. The courts are reluctant to make artificial assumptions about the term after review unless driven to this by the express words of the review clause. In other words, the parties are taken to have intended that the hypothetical lease is to be a letting on the same terms (other than rent) as those contained in the actual lease.

The clause will also include the requisite machinery for review (ie provide the procedure necessary for the initiation of the review process and set out certain time limits for the determination of any dispute as to the rent by an arbitrator or expert). It is common for the rent review to be initiated by a landlord's notice of review (a trigger notice) served on the tenant. Less commonly, the review process may be automatic, for example, where the clause provides for the new rent to be agreed between the parties (or determined by arbitration) at any time before the review date specified in the lease. If a notice procedure is provided for, the clause will normally require the tenant to serve a counternotice in response to the landlord's notice triggering the review. There may also be provisions for the service of further notices requiring arbitration which may be served by either party, if they cannot agree on a new rent within a specified time. Usually, such a notice requires the

President of the RICS to appoint a valuer to act as an arbitrator or expert.

In the absence of any contra-indications, it is presumed that time is not of the essence of a review clause: *United Scientific Holdings Ltd v Burnley Borough Council* (1978). When time is not of the essence, the mere fact that the landlord has delayed beyond the review date in initiating the review will not of itself entitle the tenant to claim that the right to review has been lost. It is, of course, open to the parties to make time of the essence so that failure to serve a notice on time will prevent the initiation of the review, or an effective response to it by the tenant or the appointment of an arbitrator or expert. Time is also presumed to be of the essence where the review notice procedure is clearly interrelated with the exercise by the tenant of an option to determine the lease. Especially where a time interval is provided for in the lease between the last date for service of the landlord's notice and the exercise of the tenant's right to determine, the parties are taken to have intended that the tenant is to know that a rent review has been initiated and what the likely review rent will be, before deciding whether to break the lease. Time will also be of the essence if the parties clearly provide for the consequences if no rent review is invoked by a certain date. For example, the clause may require the landlord to state in his trigger notice a fixed figure as the new rent payable, which will automatically take effect as such unless challenged by the tenant within a specified period.

The courts, in interpreting review clauses, seek to give effect to the intention of the parties and the principle of 'reality' applies in that it is presumed that the parties did not intend to produce an artificial result, nor one which would confer on the landlord any extra benefits beyond an uplift of the current rent at the date of review. For example, whether a rent review operates retrospectively is a matter of construction of the relevant clause. The general presumption is that the new revised rent is payable from the next quarter day following the review and not as from the date for the review specified in the lease. A clear provision is required to rebut this presumption.

In default of agreement between the parties, the review clause will provide for the appointment of an arbitrator or independent expert to determine the new revised rent. An arbitration is subject to the provisions of the Arbitration Act 1996. An appeal lies on a question of law to the High Court against an arbitration award unless the parties have otherwise agreed: s 69(1) of the 1996 Act. An appeal is only available with the agreement of all the parties to the arbitration proceedings or with leave of the court. Leave to appeal will only be given if the court is satisfied that the decision of the arbitrator is 'obviously wrong' or the question is one of general public importance and the arbitrator's decision 'is at least open to serious doubt': s69(3). In addition, (a) the determination of the question must substantially affect the rights of one or more of the parties; (b) the question is one which the arbitrator was asked to determine; and (c) despite the agreement of the parties to resolve the matter by arbitration, it is just and proper in all the circumstances for the court to determine the question. The High Court may confirm, vary or set aside the award or remit it for reconsideration by the arbitrator in the light of the court's determination on the question of law. Unless the High Court or Court of Appeal gives leave, and it is certified by the High Court that the question of law is one of general public importance, no further appeal lies to the Court of Appeal from the High Court: s69(8).

In addition to an appeal on a question of law against an arbitrator's award, there is a different route for an aggrieved party under s60 of the Arbitration Act 1996. A party to the arbitration proceedings may apply to the High Court challenging the award on the ground of 'serious irregularity' affecting the award: s68(1). A serious irregularity is defined as meaning an irregularity which the court considers has caused (or will cause) substantial injustice to the applicant and includes: (a) the arbitrator exceeding his powers; (b) failure by the arbitrator to conduct the proceedings in accordance with the procedure agreed by the parties; (c) failure by the arbitrator to deal with the issues that were put to him; (d) uncertainty or ambiguity as to the effect of the award; or (e) the award being obtained by fraud or the award (or the way in which it was procured) being contrary to public policy: s68(2).

The rent review clause may, alternatively, require that if the parties cannot agree on the new rent, it is to be determined by a valuer or surveyor acting as an independent expert. In such cases, the Arbitration Act procedure has no application. The expert is entitled to use his own expertise and to form his own judgment, and his determination can only be set aside in very limited circumstances. In *National Grid Co plc* v *M25 Group Ltd* (1999), it was held that, whilst it was open to the parties to expressly exclude the jurisdiction of the court, in the absence of such exclusion the lease will generally be construed as giving the court power to determine whether the expert has acted outside the parties' agreed parameters and applied the wrong basis for valuation. Thus, if the expert mis-construes the parties' pre-agreed valuation guidelines and conducts the valuation on a basis not provided by the parties, it is open to the court to intervene by declaring the determination a nullity.

2.1.6 Remedies for non-payment of rent

When faced with a tenant who has fallen into rent arrears, the landlord will have several remedies available to him:

- *Rent action*. The action for rent is a debt action founded in contract. It is noteworthy that the landlord may be able to pursue several persons, collectively or singularly, for outstanding rent. Thus, if the defaulting tenant is an assignee of the lease, the landlord may be able to pursue the original tenant (instead of the assignee) in contract for the arrears and/or any guarantor of the tenant. In respect of leases granted before 1 January 1996, an original tenant remains liable in contract for the default of the assignee by virtue of the doctrine of privity of contract. However, the landlord may only claim the arrears from the original tenant by serving an appropriate notice of arrears: see further Ch 6, at p78. Moreover, the landlord's ability to sue the original tenant for the default of an assignee is severely curtailed in respect of leases granted on or after 1 January 1996, by virtue of the Landlord and Tenant (Covenants) Act 1995: see Ch 6;
- *Forfeiture of the lease*. Where there are rent arrears under a fixed term lease, the landlord may, in addition to seeking payment of the arrears, elect to terminate the lease by initiating forfeiture proceedings against the tenant if the lease contains a clause entitling him to do so. In practical terms, most (if not all modern commercial leases) contain such a clause. There are complicated statutory provisions which entitle the tenant, in most circumstan-ces, to apply for relief from forfeiture, upon tendering the unpaid rent and the landlord's costs of the action. The forfeiture of a lease for non-payment of rent is discussed in Chapter 7, at 7.2;
- *Levying distress*. The remedy of distress for rent is a self-help remedy which entitles the landlord to recover unpaid rent by seizing possession of the tenant's goods and selling the same in order to raise a sufficient amount of money to pay off the rent owing. The remedy entitles the landlord to physically enter the demised premises and seize chattels to the value of the rent owing. If, within five days following seizure, no rent is forthcoming from

the tenant, the goods may be sold at auction. The Law of Distress Amendment Act 1888 enables a court to approve and appoint a bailiff to carry out the distraint of the tenant's chattels. If a bailiff is appointed, the tenant must be given notice of the distress by such bailiff. Once seized, goods subject to the distraint can be impounded prior to sale and, thereafter, be sold five or more days after the service of any notice of distress. If the tenant interferes with any goods seized, he will be guilty of 'pound breach'. If this occurs, the landlord is entitled to recapture the goods and may claim damages from the tenant in compensation for the pound breach. In the event, however, that the landlord wrongfully exercises his self-help remedy of distress, the tenant is entitled to similarly exercise a self-help counter-remedy of 'rescue' before such time as the goods are impounded or, alternatively, bring an action in the County Court for the return of the goods any time prior to sale. Certain chattels of the tenant are exempt from the remedy of distress (eg tenant's fixtures, loose money, tools of the tenant's trade): see Distress for Rent Act 1689.

2.2 Insurance

The lease will invariably provide for either the landlord or tenant to execute a policy of insurance for the demised premises against such risks as fire, flood, lightning, vandalism, terrorism, etc. Often, it will be the landlord who covenants to insure, but it is the tenant who will bear the burden of meeting the cost of the insurance premiums which (as already mentioned earlier) are often made payable as additional rent. In such cases, the courts will not imply a term to the effect that the landlord should safeguard the tenant's financial interests by placing the insurance with the insurer who provides the lowest quotation: see *Bandar Property Holdings Ltd* v *JS Darwen (Successors) Ltd* (1968). The decision in *Bandar* was followed in *Havenridge Ltd* v *Boston Dyers Ltd* (1994), where the Court of Appeal reiterated the principle that it was sufficient for the landlord to prove that the premium paid was no greater than the going rate for that insurer in the normal course of his business at the time.

On occasion, where the tenant has undertaken to effect the necessary insurance cover for the property, the landlord reserves in his own favour a power of veto as to the appropriateness of the insurer in question. In such cases, the landlord's power of veto is valid and the landlord's consent is a condition precedent to the insurance being effected. Moreover, in the absence of any express

provision to the contrary, the landlord is not under any obligation
to act reasonably in the withholding of consent: *Tredegar (Viscount)
v Harwood* (1929).

If the premises are destroyed or damaged, for example, by fire,
the question of the application of the insurance moneys can often
pose difficult problems between the parties. In *Re King, (Deceased)
Robinson v Gray* (1963), the tenant covenanted to keep the premises
in repair; at her own expense, to insure the premises against fire in
the joint names of the landlord and tenant; and to apply the
insurance moneys in rebuilding. When the premises were
destroyed by fire, the insurance moneys were paid in the joint
names of the parties, but reinstatement was not possible owing to a
local authority's compulsory acquisition of the property. The Court
of Appeal held that the tenant was entitled to the whole of the
insurance moneys since the landlord's only interest therein was as
security for the performance by the tenant of her obligations to
repair and reinstate and that, as the premium had been paid by the
tenant to meet her obligations, the moneys belonged to her.

In *Beacon Carpets Ltd v Kirby* (1984), the insurance moneys under
a policy effected by the landlord in the joint names of the parties for
their 'respective rights and interests' proved insufficient to pay for
full reinstatement after a fire destroyed the building. The Court of
Appeal held that the basic right of the parties was to have the
insurance moneys applied in rebuilding for their respective benefit.
However, because the parties had by their own acts released that
right without agreeing how the moneys were to be dealt with, it
could only be inferred that, in default of agreement, they were
treating the insurance moneys as standing in the place of the
building which would otherwise have been replaced. It followed
that the insurance moneys belonged to the parties in shares pro-
portionate to their respective interests in the property insured. The
case of *Re King* (above) was distinguished, since that case dealt only
with the rights in the insurance moneys once the prime purpose of
rebuilding had been frustrated by the actions of a third party, and
did not affect the case (as in *Beacon*) where the parties were treating
the insurance moneys as standing in the place of the building.

Where the landlord's obligation to insure is satisfied at the
tenant's expense, it will endure for the benefit of *both* the landlord
and the tenant and, accordingly, the landlord will be obliged to use
the insurance moneys, if called upon to do so, towards the
reinstatement of the demised premises. In *Mumford Hotels Ltd v
Wheler* (1964), the lease did not contain an express covenant to

reinstate. When the premises were destroyed by fire, the insurance moneys were paid to the landlord, who refused to reinstate the property. The Court held that the issue was not whether a covenant to reinstate should be implied, but whether the true inference was that the landlord should be treated as insuring on her own behalf or for the joint benefit of herself and the tenant. In the circumstances, the landlord's obligation to insure, at the tenant's expense, was intended to be for the benefit of both parties, so that the landlord was obliged to use the insurance moneys to reinstate the premises if called upon to do so.

The Fires Prevention (Metropolis) Act 1774, s83, provides that where the demised premises are burnt down, demolished or damaged by fire, the party who has not expressly covenanted to insure the property (eg the tenant) may require the insurance moneys paid to the insuring party (eg the landlord) to be spent on the reinstatement of the premises. In *Reynolds* v *Phoenix Assurance Co Ltd* (1978), the plaintiffs had written to request that the defendant insurers lay out and expend moneys towards reinstating the fire damaged premises. They made this request in order to bring into effect the provisions of the 1774 Act. The Court, however, held that the Act was intended to deal with a different situation, namely, to prevent insurance moneys being paid to an insured (eg the landlord) who might make away with them. It was not intended to apply to a case where the insured and the person serving the notice were one and the same person.

In the event that property has been demised to the tenant on a full-repairing lease, and the premises have been destroyed by fire with no notice having been served under the 1774 Act, it seems that the tenant, in the absence of express provision, has no equity to compel his landlord to expend the insurance moneys on the demised premises: *Leeds* v *Cheetham* (1827). Such a tenant also remains bound, despite the fire, to abide by his own repairing and rental obligations. However, today, developments in the doctrine of frustration may offer the tenant a remedy in this regard: *National Carriers Ltd* v *Panalpina (Northern) Ltd* (1981); see Ch 7, at 7.9. From the standpoint of the tenant, it would seem sensible to include an express covenant for insurance moneys to be applied towards reinstatement in the lease in order to cover such an eventuality.

The tenant usually covenants not to do anything which would increase the insurance premiums or avoid the policy. A covenant to insure is broken if at any time the premises are uninsured (or not insured to the value specified), irrespective of whether any damage is caused. The measure of damages for breach of the covenant to insure is the actual loss incurred. For example, if the tenant fails to insure in breach of covenant and the landlord does so, the landlord will be entitled to recover the premiums by way of damages. If the premises are damaged, and in breach of covenant they are not insured, the damages recoverable will represent the full cost of reinstatement up to the sum which ought to have been insured.

2.3 Service charges

It is now common for a commercial lease of an office block, industrial park or indoor shopping centre to contain a service charge provision. The modern trend is towards 'clear leases' under which all expenditure relating to the premises is passed on to the various tenants within the development.

The service charge clause will place the burden of repair, maintenance of common parts, insurance, air conditioning, service staff, etc, on the landlord. Normally, the landlord will expressly covenant with the tenant to perform these services. In some clauses, however, performance by the landlord is merely a condition precedent of the tenant's obligation to pay the service charge. In other words, if the landlord does not perform the services, the tenant's obligation to pay does not arise. In the absence of an express covenant, the tenant may find it difficult to compel the landlord to provide the various services.

It is usual for the landlord's obligation to be qualified so as not to render him liable if performance becomes impossible due to circumstances beyond his control (eg mechanical failure or shortage of fuel). Invariably, the clause will provide that the landlord is to use his best or reasonable endeavours to supply the service and that the service will be carried out with reasonable care and skill.

The primary aim of the service charge from the landlord's standpoint is, of course, to provide him with complete reimbursement for all his expenditure in maintaining and servicing the premises. It is important, therefore, that the service charge covers exactly all the expenditure which the landlord has undertaken to perform. Obviously, not all expenditure will be recoverable under a service charge provision since some works will fall outside the definition of 'repair' or 'maintenance' and constitute an improvement to the property. For example, in *Mullaney* v *Maybourne Grange (Croydon) Management Co Ltd* (1986), the landlord was held not entitled to recover expenditure on replacing windows since the work went beyond repair and the new windows could not be regarded as an 'additional amenity' within the service charge clause. It is important that the clause also covers the landlord's expenses of managing the premises (ie the cost of employing managing agents) and this is normally done by obliging each tenant to pay a stated percentage of the service charge (thereby imposing a ceiling on such expenses).

The question of apportionment of the total expenditure between the various tenants may give rise to some difficulty. There are a number of methods of apportionment commonly adopted:

- *Fixed proportion*. This involves allocating a fixed percentage of the service charge to each unit within the development;
- *Floor space*. This method of apportionment is based on the floor space ratios between the different units. The major problem with this method is that it may unduly favour tenants of small units at the expense of tenants of larger units. This is usually overcome by providing for a weighted floor space proportion;
- *User of services*. This is considered the fairest method since it is based on a yearly calculation of the actual benefit derived from each service by each tenant within the development. It does, however, involve complex calculations which will be wholly impracticable in most cases;
- *Fair proportion*. Here, the tenant's service charge contribution is based on a fair proportion (determined by a surveyor) of the landlord's expenditure.

The service charge clause will usually provide a procedure for certification of the landlord's expenditure. The most common method adopted is to require the landlord to produce certified accounts at the end of each financial year. The usual practice is for the certification to be carried out by a surveyor or accountant. The issue of such a certificate is normally treated as a condition precedent of the tenant's liability to pay the service charge: *Finchbourne Ltd* v *Rodrigues* (1976). The landlord will be most concerned to prevent challenges to the certificate based on arguments that the expenditure is excessive or unreasonable. It is possible to expressly exclude challenges on this ground, but the more usual practice is to have such challenges referred to an independent arbitrator or expert for his determination. In *Berrycroft Management Co Ltd* v *Sinclair Gardens Investments (Kensington) Ltd* (1997), it was held that a term could not be implied that the sum charged by the nominated insurer should not be unreasonable, or that a tenant should not be required to pay a substantially higher sum than he could himself arrange with an insurance office of repute. In this case, the right of the landlord to nominate the insurance company was unqualified so the fact that the tenants could have secured lower rates was immaterial.

The service charge clause will normally provide for the making of interim payments so as to enable the landlord to meet expenditure as it falls due during the year. An adjustment is made when the actual service charge is known, either by the tenant paying the difference, or by the landlord making an allowance. Provision may also be made for a reserve fund to cover unforeseen expenditure (eg replacement of a central heating system). Such a reserve fund is normally placed in a separate interest-bearing deposit account or on trust for the contributing tenants.

The service charge element is usually expressed in the lease as additional rent thereby enabling the landlord to levy distress against any amounts outstanding (see above). However, this will also give the tenant the ability to seek relief if the landlord seeks to forfeit the lease for non-payment of rent (including service charge): *Escalus Properties Ltd* v *Robinson* (1995).

Chapter 3

Disrepair

3.1 Introduction

A commercial lease will inevitably contain express covenants to repair the demised property. Although there are also some implied obligations in respect of the state and condition of the premises on both the landlord and tenant in the commercial context, the parties will invariably turn to the covenants in the lease in order to determine the precise extent and scope of their respective repairing liabilities.

3.2 General principles of construction

Problems of interpretation frequently arise in the context of a repairing covenant in a lease where the parties have sought to define their respective obligations in regard to the maintenance and upkeep of the property. The correct approach to interpretation is to adhere, as nearly as possible, to the express words which are found in the covenant and to give those words a commercially sensible or a reasonable commercial interpretaion. The words are not necessarily to be given their strict literal meaning since, in all cases, it is the 'good sense of the agreement' which has to be ascertained. For example, a covenant 'forthwith' to put premises in repair must receive a reasonable construction and cannot be construed in its strict literal sense. Accordingly, the word 'forthwith' means with all reasonable speed and not necessarily 'immediately'.

The meaning of a particular phrase or expression intended by the parties must, in the first instance, be construed by reference to the actual terms of the lease itself. Thus, where the precise purport and scope of a covenant is plain from the express words used, it is not permissible to look beyond the lease in which the covenant is contained. But if a doubt still remains as to the precise meaning, regard may be had to the surrounding circumstances with reference to which the lease was entered into. The surrounding circumstances include the nature of the property and the purpose for which it is suitable but not the past history of the matter, the conduct of the parties or the statements of their intention.

3.2.1 *The meaning of particular words and phrases*

The courts have interpreted particular expressions commonly used in repairing covenants as follows:

- *'To keep in repair'*. A tenant who has covenanted to 'repair and keep in repair' the demised premises during the term must have them in repair at all times during the term and so, if they are at any time out of repair, he commits a breach of the covenant. Consequently, the covenant obliges the tenant to put the premises in repair (if they are not in repair when the lease begins) and to leave them in repair during the currency of the term: *Credit Suisse* v *Beegas Nominees Ltd* (1994);
- *'To leave/deliver up in repair'*. Under this wording when used alone, no liability can arise on the part of the tenant until the end of the term;
- *'To put into repair forthwith'*. A covenant to put premises into repair 'forthwith' is performed if the repairs are done with reasonable speed;
- *'Repair in the [fourth] year of the term'*. Here, the tenant's liability will arise as soon as the specified year commences;
- *'Repair, good repair, tenantable repair, substantial repair'*. All these expressions mean repair to the standard laid down by Lopes LJ in *Proudfoot* v *Hart* (1890), namely, 'such repair as, having regard to the age, character and locality of the house, would make it reasonably fit for the occupation of a reasonably minded tenant of the class who would be likely to take it'. The standard of repair is measured by reference to the parties' contemplation regarding the age, nature and condition of the premises at the time when the lease was executed and when the covenant began to operate. Thus, where the premises are old at the time of the demise, the tenant need only maintain them in a fit state of repair as old premises. He is under no obligation to bring the premises up to date;
- *'To repair and renew'*. This is no wider than a covenant to repair, because stronger and clearer words are necessary to impose a larger and more onerous obligation: see *Collins* v *Flynn* (1963);
- *'Structural repairs'*. These are repairs which involve interference with or alteration to the essential structure, fabric or framework

of the building in question, including the walls (external and internal, supporting or load-bearing), roof, foundations, floors, etc. In *Smedley* v *Chumley & Hawke Ltd* (1981), the lease of a restaurant forming part of a motel complex contained a tenant's covenant to repair the interior and exterior of the demised premises, and a landlord's covenant to keep the main walls and roof in good structural condition and repair throughout the tenancy. A few years after the commencement of the lease, it became evident that the foundations of the restaurant were defective. The Court of Appeal held that the landlords were liable under the covenant. The only way to put the walls and roof into a safe, structural condition was to carry out such major works to the foundations as were necessary to give the walls a stable base. Certainly, however, mere decorative repairs (see 3.3) cannot be regarded as structural because these will not interfere with the main structural framework or fabric of the demised property;

- **'Exterior'.** This word has been held to include windows and skylights, outside drains, flagstones and steps, and the roof. But the word 'exterior' does not necessarily include the roof of a building where the demise includes the top floor of a building but not the roof itself. In *Campden Hill Towers* v *Gardner* (1977), the word 'exterior' in the context of (what is now) s11 of the Landlord and Tenant Act 1985, when applied to a flat separately occupied within a block of flats, extended to that part of the outside wall of the block which constituted a wall of the flat, to its other outside wall or walls, the outside of its inner party walls, the outsides of horizontal divisions between the flat and those above and below, and the structural framework and beams directly supporting its walls, ceilings and floors. Although the case involved a residential block of flats, similar principles would, no doubt, apply to commercial accommodation (eg in an office block);

- **'Fair wear and tear excepted'.** When this expression is used in a repairing covenant, the tenant is not bound to make good dilapidations caused by the friction of air and by exposure and ordinary use. The tenant, however, is not released from his obligation to repair anything which has become damaged as a direct consequence of a defect originally proceeding from reasonable wear and tear. Consequential damage, therefore, does not come within the 'fair wear and tear' exclusion and the tenant will be liable for its repair under his covenant.

3.3 Decorative repairs

As a general rule, a repairing covenant does not carry with it the obligation to carry out decorative repairs except painting necessary for the prevention of decay as opposed to mere ornamentation. In *Crayford v Newton* (1886), the Court of Appeal held that a tenant who agreed to keep the inside of the premises in tenantable repair, and who occupied them for 17 years without having painted or papered, was only bound to paint and paper so as to prevent the house from going into decay. In *Proudfoot v Hart* (1890), however, the Court of Appeal, whilst laying down the general rule that the tenant is not bound by a general repairing covenant to do repairs which are merely decorative, also concluded that he is bound to repaper, paint etc walls and ceilings if the condition of the property in those respects is such that it would not be taken by a reasonably minded tenant of the class likely to take it.

Most leases will contain a separate covenant to paint at stated periods during the term so as to ensure liability on the tenant in respect of decorative order. However, a tenant may be able to avail himself of the special form of relief available in respect of *internal* decorative repairs under s147 of the Law of Property Act 1925, which provides that the court may relieve the tenant from liability for such repairs if, having regard to all the circumstances of the case (including, in particular, the length of the tenant's term), the court is satisfied that the landlord's notice requiring the work is unreasonable.

Covenants to repair, paint etc must also be construed reasonably so that the landlord is not entitled to claim for slight defects. In *Perry v Chotzner* (1893), it was held that, under a covenant to repair and paint, the tenant was not bound to fill up cracks in plaster and holes made by nails within the period of redecorating.

3.4 The extent of the demised premises

The precise physical extent of the demised premises is particularly relevant in the context of construing the exact effect of repairing obligations. Traditionally, lawyers have always tended to define the demised premises by reference to a verbal description and also a plan. Unfortunately, most plans tend to be small-scale or inaccurate drawings which are of little assistance in determining the precise physical boundary of a repairing liability. It should also be borne in mind that the wording used by the draftsman will dictate the role of any plan: if he uses the words 'for identification purposes only', then the verbal description will prevail over any inconsistent plan; if he uses the words 'more particularly delineated', then the plan will prevail over the verbal description.

3.5 Repair contrasted with improvement

The test to be applied in determining whether particular works can properly be described as 'repair' (as opposed to works of improvement) is whether they involve giving back to the landlord a wholly different thing from that demised under the lease. In deciding this question, regard may be had, as a guide, to the proportion which the cost of the works bear to the value of the whole of the premises. However, in a situation where the value of the demised building when repaired is very much less than the cost of putting up a new building altogether, it is the cost of putting up the new building (not the value of the old building when repaired), which should be compared with the cost of the works required to repair the old building. In *Elite Investments Ltd* v *TI Bainbridge Silencers Ltd* (1986), a lease of an industrial unit contained a general repairing covenant on the part of the tenant. At the date of the lease, the roof was already deteriorating and, by the date of the hearing, it was beyond patching and needed to be entirely replaced. Replacement of the roof would cost £84,364. In its dilapidated condition, the unit had virtually no value for lettings, but its value as repaired would be about £140,000–£150,000. However, the cost of re-erecting the building was estimated at approximately £1 million. The Court held that the replacement of the roof constituted a repair or replacement of part of the demised premises within the meaning of the tenant's covenant. The unit would not be a different thing but merely an industrial building with a new roof.

A repair may include the remedying of an inherent defect in the design or construction of the property. The essential question is whether, having regard to all the circumstances of the case, the proposed remedial works can fairly be regarded as 'repair' in the context of the particular lease. In *Ravenseft Properties Ltd* v *Davstone (Holdings) Ltd* (1980), a building, consisting of a 16-storey block of maisonettes, was constructed of a reinforced concrete frame with stone claddings. Expansion joints were omitted from the structure because at the date of construction (1958–1960) it was not standard practice to include them. In 1966, the tenant took a lease of the building. The lease contained a tenant's covenant to repair. In 1973, part of the stone cladding on the building became loose and was in danger of falling because of bowing of the stones caused principally by the defect in design of lack of expansion joints. The cost of inserting the joints was £5,000. The cost of erecting the building in 1973 would have exceeded £3 million. The Court held that there was no doctrine that want of repair due to an inherent defect in the demised property could not fall within the ambit of a covenant to repair. It was a question of degree whether that which the tenant was asked to do, or pay for, could properly be described as a work of repair, or whether it involved giving back to the landlord a wholly different thing from that demised. The insertion of the joints did not amount to changing the character of the building so as to take the work out of the scope of the covenant to repair because the joints formed a trivial part only of the whole building and the cost of inserting them was trivial compared with the value of the building.

The word 'disrepair' connotes a deterioration from a former *better* condition so that, where there is no evidence before the court demonstrating that the condition of the property has in any way deteriorated since it was first built, no breach of the repairing covenant will be held to have occurred. For example, in *Post Office* v *Aquarius Properties Ltd* (1987), involving a newly-constructed office building, there was a defect in the structure of the basement by reason of porous concrete and defective construction joints used in the construction which caused water to enter the basement whenever the water table rose, as it did between 1979 and 1984 when the basement was ankle-deep in water. In 1984, the water table receded and the basement became dry. No damage had been caused to any part of the building by the defect, which had not been aggravated but was in the same condition as when the building was built. The Court of Appeal held that, because the building was and at all times had been in the same physical condition as it was when constructed, no want of repair had been proved for which the tenants could be liable under the covenant.

The word 'repair' has been defined as meaning the restoration by renewal or replacement of *subsidiary* parts of the whole as opposed to the reconstruction of the whole or substantially the whole: *Lurcott* v *Wakeley* (1911). In *Morcom* v *Campbell-Johnson* (1956), Denning LJ described the difference between repair and improvement in the following terms:

> If the work which is done is the provision of something new for the benefit of the occupier, that is, properly speaking, an improvement; but

if it is only the replacement of something already there, which has become dilapidated or worn out, then albeit that it is the replacement by its modern equivalent, it comes within the category of repairs and not improvements.

By way of summary, it may be said that the following criteria have been established for determining whether a work constitutes a repair, namely:

- Whether the works go to the whole or substantially the whole of the structure, or only to a subsidiary part;
- Whether the effect is to produce a building of a wholly different character from that which had been let; and
- What is the cost of the works in relation to the value or cost of the building.

If the tenant is liable to repair under his repairing covenant, he must execute the remedial works in accordance with modern building standards: *Ravenseft Properties Ltd v Davstone (Holdings) Ltd* (1980). In *Creska Ltd v Hammersmith and Fulham London Borough Council* (1998), the landlord was obliged to install a modern under-floor heating system in place of the old defective system even though this would incorporate some improvements in design.

3.6 Notice of the disrepair

In some leases, an obligation to repair will be placed on the landlord. The landlord's liability may be restricted to the external parts or common areas of the building, or extend to the whole property. The general rule is that a covenant to keep premises in repair obliges the landlord to keep them in repair at all times, so that there is a breach of the obligation immediately a defect occurs. In *British Telecommunications plc v Sun Life Assurance Society plc* (1995), the plaintiff company was the tenant of premises on the sixth and seventh floors of a building under a lease which required the defendant company, as landlord, to keep the building as a whole in 'complete good and substantial repair and condition'. A bulge appeared in the brick cladding forming part of the external walls at fifth floor level. The landlord was later informed of the defect and immediately took steps to safeguard the walls preparatory to carrying out the necessary remedial work. The issue was whether the landlord became liable immediately the bulge in the cladding appeared (as contended by the tenant) or only on the expiration of a reasonable period for doing the repairs following the appearance of the defect. The Court of Appeal held that there was a breach of the covenant as soon as the defect occurred.

If, however, the defect occurs in the demised premises, the landlord is only liable when he has notice of the defect in question: *O'Brien* v *Robinson* (1973). As to what constitutes sufficient notice, it is evident that the tenant is not obliged to identify the precise nature or degree of the disrepair to his landlord: see eg *Griffin* v *Pillet* (1926), where the tenant's letter to the landlord stating merely that 'the steps to the front door want attention' was held good notice. Actual knowledge, or information about the existence of a defect such as would put a reasonable man on inquiry as to whether works of repair were needed, is also sufficient for the landlord's obligation to commence: *Sheldon* v *West Bromwich Corporation* (1973). It is sufficient if the landlord is given notification of the defect through his agent (eg rent collector, officer or employee): *Dinefwr Borough Council* v *Jones* (1987) and *Hall* v *Howard* (1988). The notice rule requires the landlord to execute the remedial works within a reasonable period of time from being given notice of the defect. What is a reasonable time is, of course, a question of fact depending on the urgency of the required repairs.

The requirement of prior notice may also apply where a defect is caused by an occurrence wholly outside the landlord's control (eg where the roof of a building is damaged by a branch from a tree standing on neighbouring land not in the possession or control of the landlord and rainwater finds its way into the tenant's premises by that means). There are, however, judicial decisions where landlords have been held liable for breach of covenant though the cause of the defect was fortuitous and occurred through no fault on their part: see eg *Bishop* v *Consolidated London Properties Ltd* (1933).

3.7 Implied obligations to repair

Although there are a number of implied obligations on the landlord (both under the common law and statute) in relation to the state and condition of the demised property, most of these are confined to residential accommodation and, therefore, have no relevance to commercial premises (eg fitness for human habitation and liability to repair the structure and exterior of the dwelling-house under ss 8 and 11 of the Landlord and Tenant Act 1985). The following implied obligations, however, apply in the commercial context as well:

- The landlord is under an implied common law obligation to maintain to a reasonable standard the essential means of access/common parts to units in a building in multiple accommodation: *Liverpool City Council* v *Irwin* (1977). The court may, however, refuse to imply such a term against a landlord of commercial premises where the lease contains perfectly adequate repairing covenants on the part of both landlord and tenant: *Duke of Westminster* v *Guild* (1985). In *Wettern Electric Ltd* v *Welsh Development Agency* (1983), the Court held that a term as to fitness for purpose could be implied in a licence to occupy commercial property on the basis of the *Irwin* decision;

- An obligation to repair may also be implied at common law on the landlord in order to match a correlative obligation on the part of the tenant. In *Barrett* v *Lounova (1982) Ltd* (1990), the Court of Appeal held that, since the tenant's covenant to keep the interior of the premises in good repair would eventually become impossible to perform in the absence of a corresponding obligation to repair the exterior, it was necessary (in order to give business efficacy to the tenancy agreement) to impose an obligation to carry out exterior repairs on the landlord. However, in the context of a long lease which deals expressly with repair and imposes an insurance obligation to cover catastrophic damage to the building, there will be no basis on which to presume any intention that the landlord should be obliged to repair the structure of the building: *Adami* v *Lincoln Grange Management Ltd* (1998).

3.8 Liability in tort

The landlord may also be liable in tort for defects in the premises as a result of his negligence. Thus, a landlord who designs and/or builds premises owes a common law duty of care to take reasonable steps to ensure that the premises are reasonably safe: *Rimmer* v *Liverpool City Council* (1985). Under s4(1) of the Defective Premises Act 1972, the landlord, who has covenanted to repair, is under an obligation to the tenant (and third parties) to keep them 'reasonably safe from personal injury or from damage to their property' caused by defects in the state of the premises. Although s4(1) is concerned with a landlord who is in breach of his own repairing covenant, s4(4) of the Act also operates to impose liability on a landlord despite the fact that, under the terms of the tenancy,

it is the tenant who is obliged to repair. In *McAuley* v *Bristol City Council* (1992), the Court of Appeal held that s4(4) of the 1972 Act imposes a duty of care on a landlord towards his tenant (and others) where premises are let under a tenancy which expressly or impliedly gives the landlord the right to enter the premises to carry out any description of maintenance or repair of the premises.

Where the landlord retains in his possession and control something ancillary to the demised premises (eg a roof or staircase), the maintenance of which in proper repair is necessary for the protection of the demised premises or the safe enjoyment of them by the tenant, the landlord is under an obligation to take reasonable care that the premises retained in his occupation are not in such a condition as to cause damage to the tenant or the demised property: *Duke of Westminster* v *Guild* (1985).

So far as the tenant is concerned, an implied liability to repair may arise under the tort of waste or nuisance, or under the Occupiers' Liability Act 1957. In addition, there is an implied obligation on the tenant to use the premises in a tenant-like manner: *Warren* v *Keen* (1954). This latter obligation requires the tenant to keep proper care of the property and not deliberately damage it, and is not, strictly speaking, a covenant to repair, although the tenant may be obliged to carry out small jobs (eg unblock the sink), of the kind that a reasonable tenant would do.

3.9 Remedies for breach of a repairing obligation

3.9.1 *Landlord's remedies*

The following is a list of landlord's remedies against a tenant who is in breach of his covenant to repair:

- *Damages.* The measure of damages differs according to whether the landlord's claim is brought during the currency of the lease or upon its expiry. Where the action is brought during the currency of the lease, the damages will represent the amount by which the landlord's reversion has depreciated in marketable value by the premises being out of repair. Practically, this is the amount by which the saleable value of the premises is reduced by the neglect bearing in mind the length of the unexpired term. By s18(1) of the Landlord and Tenant Act 1927, however, damages for breach of a covenant during the currency of the term cannot exceed the amount (if any) by which the value of the premises is reduced. Therefore, this provides an upper limit to the amount of damages recoverable by the landlord. While the cost of repairs may be an aid in the assessment, it should be scaled down according to the length of the remaining term of the lease. Thus, the nearer the end of the term, the more important the cost of the repairs becomes as evidence of damage to the reversion.

At the end of the term, the landlord may bring an action on the covenant to yield up the premises in repair. The measure of damages is the amount necessary to put the premises into the condition in which they should have been left in accordance with the repairing covenant, bearing in mind the class of property and its age. Further, the landlord is entitled to compensation for the loss of the use of the property while the repair is being done. The effect of s18(1) of the Landlord and Tenant Act 1927 (see above) is that the common law measure of damages now equates with the extent to which the value of the landlord's reversion has been diminished;

• *Forfeiture of the lease.* A landlord faced with a tenant who is in breach of his covenant to repair will need to elect whether to forfeit the lease or, alternatively, waive the right to forfeit by treating the lease as continuing and rest content with a claim for damages only. In virtually all cases (other than non-payment of rent) a prerequisite to forfeiture is the service by the landlord of a notice under s146 of the Law of Property Act 1925: see Ch 7, at 7.2. He must, in the notice, specify the particular breach complained of and, if the breach is capable of remedy, require the tenant to remedy the same within a reasonable time. In addition, where appropriate, the notice must refer to the landlord's claim for damages. The s146 notice need not itself specify the precise time within which the breach of covenant must be remedied, and it is usual practice simply to require the tenant to remedy within a 'reasonable time' from the date of the service of the notice. It will then be a matter for the landlord's surveyor/solicitor to advise his client on what period of time can safely be allowed to elapse before the commencement of proceedings for forfeiture. His advice will, no doubt, take into account such matters as the extent and nature of the disrepair, the time of year and the availability of builders. It is usual to particularise the breach(es) complained of by means of annexing to the notice a schedule of dilapidations prepared by the landlord's surveyor.

When the lease is question was granted for seven or more years, and three years or more remain unexpired at the date of the s146 notice, the landlord's remedies of forfeiture (and damages) are limited by the provisions of the Leasehold Property (Repairs) Act 1938. Where the Act applies, the landlord cannot proceed without first serving a s146 notice, which must inform the tenant of his right to serve a counternotice claiming the benefit of the Act. If the tenant does serve such a counternotice within 28 days, no further proceedings by action or otherwise (ie by initiating proceedings for possesssion or by physically re-entering upon the premises) can be taken by the landlord without leave of the court establishing a case (on the balance of probabilities) that one or more of the five grounds set out in the Act have been fulfilled: see *Associated British Ports* v *CH Bailey plc* (1990). The five grounds are: (a) the value of the reversion has been substantially diminished or will be if the breach is not immediately remedied; (b) immediate remedying is required by any Act, byelaw, court order or local authority order; (c) immediate remedying is required in the interest of an occupier (of the whole or part) other than the tenant; (d) the cost of immediate remedying is relatively small in comparison with the likely cost if the work is postponed; and (e) special circumstances which in the opinion of the court render it just and equitable that leave should be given.

Under s146(2) of the Law of Property Act 1925, the tenant is entitled to apply to the court for relief against forfeiture: see Ch 7, at 7.2.5. The court may grant or refuse relief, on terms, as it thinks fit and, in the case of a breach of a repairing covenant, the court will usually require the tenant to remedy the disrepair and make compensation to the landlord for any damage to the reversion before it grants such relief. (It should also be noted that a special form of relief is available to the tenant in respect of internal decorative repairs under s147 of the Law of Property Act 1925, see 3.3 above);

- *Injunction/specific performance*. Until recently, a landlord could not compel his tenant by mandatory injunction or specific performance to perform his repairing obligations. The law has recently changed on this point and the position now is that a tenant's repairing covenant is specifically enforceable, although it will only be in a rare case that this kind of remedy will be successfully employed against the tenant: see *Rainbow Estates Ltd* v *Tokenhold Ltd* (1998). This is because, in the context of a commercial lease, the landlord will normally have the right to forfeit the lease or to enter and do the repairs at the expense of the tenant (see below). Moreover, the courts will be astute to avoid injustice or oppression to the tenant and the remedy is likely to be confined to cases where damages are not an adequate remedy. As in the *Rainbow* case itself, this form of relief may take on an important significance if the landlord has no right of access to the demised property to carry out urgent repairs and the property is in a continuing state of deterioration. The remedy of a mandatory injunction has been denied in other contexts: see for example *Co-operative Insurance Society Ltd* v *Argyll Stores (Holdings) Ltd* (1997), where the House of Lords held that a covenant in a lease of retail premises to keep open for trade during the usual hours of business was not, save in exceptional circumstances, specifically enforceable, since it was the settled practice of the court not to make an order requiring a person to carry on a business;

- *Self-help*. The landlord will frequently have the benefit of a clause in the lease enabling him to inspect the state of repair of the demised property and serve notice on the tenant requiring him to execute the necessary repairs. If the tenant fails to do so, the landlord may carry out the work himself and recover the cost from the tenant. In these circumstances, an action by the landlord to recover the cost of the repairs is, by reason of the express terms of the clause, either a claim for a debt or rent due under the lease rather than a claim for *damages* for breach of covenant within the meaning of the Leasehold Property (Repairs) Act 1938 (see above). The practical significance of this distinction is that the landlord does not require leave under the 1938 Act to bring the action against the tenant: *Jervis* v *Harris* (1996).

Where the landlord must do urgent repairs in order to preserve the property, there is a danger of invalidating any subsequent s146 notice. In *SEDAC Investments Ltd* v *Tanner* (1982), the landlord discovered that the stonework on the front wall of the demised property was loose and in danger of falling onto passers-by. Remedial work was, therefore, undertaken by the landlord as a matter of urgency in the absence of any co-operation from the tenant who was responsible for the defect under his repairing covenant in the lease. Subsequently, the landlord served a s146 notice on the tenant. The Court held that a s146 notice to be effective had to be served before the breach complained of was remedied. Accordingly, when the landlord himself remedied the breach prior to attempting to serve the notice, he thereby put it out of his power to serve a valid s146 notice thereafter, with the consequence that the court had no jurisdiction to give him leave to commence proceedings under the 1938 Act. In cases of urgent repairs, the landlord would be advised to seek a mandatory injunction compelling the tenant to execute the remedial works without delay: see *Rainbow Estates Ltd* v *Tokenhold Ltd* (1998).

3.9.2 *Tenant's remedies*

Where the landlord is in breach of his repairing covenant in the lease, the tenant's remedies will include: damages, specific performance, termination of the letting, set-off against rent, and the appointment of a receiver. These are briefly explained below:

- *Damages*, which may be awarded under various heads of claim. These may include (a) diminution in capital or rental value to the tenant of its occupation for the relevant period: *Electricity Supply Nominees Ltd* v *National Magazine Co Ltd* (1998). If the lease has been acquired by the tenant as a saleable asset (ie if the tenant is forced by the landlord's failure to repair to sell or sublet the property at a loss), the tenant can recover the diminution of the price or recoverable rent occasioned by the failure: *Wallace* v *Manchester City Council* (1998); (b) reasonable costs incurred in renting alternative accommodation; (c) costs of redecoration and storing furniture/equipment; (d) distress, discomfort and inconvenience occasioned by the disrepair;
- *Specific performance.* In addition to damages, the tenant may seek to enforce a landlord's repairing obligation by means of a decree of specific performance. The court has an inherent equitable jurisdiction to make an order where the landlord is in possession of the land where the defect exists: *Jeune* v *Queen's Cross Properties Ltd* (1974);
- *Termination of contract of letting.* It seems that a tenancy can come to an end by the tenant's acceptance of his landlord's repudiatory breach. In *Hussein* v *Mehlman* (1992), the defendant landlord granted the plaintiff tenants an assured shorthold tenancy of a dwelling-house subject to covenants to repair implied on the part of the landlord under s11 of the Landlord and Tenant Act 1985. From the commencement of the term, the tenants made several complaints to the landlord regarding the disrepair of the premises. The landlord refused to carry out any repairs and the tenants returned the keys and vacated the property. On the evidence, the Court held that the landlord had

been guilty of a repudiatory breach (in so far as the defects rendered the house unfit to be lived in) and the tenants, by vacating the premises and returing the keys, had accepted that repudiation as putting an end to the tenancy. The case has recently been applied in the context of commercial premises. In *Nynehead Developments Ltd* v *RH Fibreboard Containers Ltd* (1999), the landlord granted the tenants a 23-year lease of commercial premises on an industrial estate. The lease granted the tenants the right to use a forecourt with other tenants, together with an exclusive right to park vehicles on part of the forecourt for the purpose of loading and unloading. It also contained a covenant on the part of the landlord 'to do whatever is reasonably incidental to the efficient operation of the industrial estate'. Subsequently, the landlord let two other units on the estate to tenants who, in breach of their leases, continually parked their vehicles on the forecourt, causing annoyance to the tenants who eventually vacated the premises. The Court held, on the facts, that the landlord's breach was not sufficiently fundamental to jutsify termination of the lease. Although the decision in *Nynehead* clarifies what constitutes a repudiatory breach in this context, a number of thorny issues remain unresolved by the courts: see Ch 7, at 7.10;

- *Set-off against rent*. By way of self-help, the tenant may opt to do the repairs himself and deduct the expense from current or future rent. On being sued for the unpaid rent by his landlord, the tenant will be able to rely on his own counterclaim against the landlord for breach of the landlord's repairing covenant as effecting a complete defence by way of an equitable set-off to the claim for rent. In addition, the tenant has a common law right to deduct the repairing cost from rent where, having given notice to the landlord, the tenant carries out the repairs which are the landlord's responsibility. The right to set-off will not be excluded where the obligation to pay rent is expressly stated in the lease to be 'without any deduction': *Connaught Restaurants Ltd* v *Indoor Leisure Ltd* (1993). Such an exclusion where operative (eg by the use of the words 'without any deduction or set-off whatsoever') does not fall foul of the Unfair Contract Terms Act 1977: *Electricity Supply Nominees Ltd* v *IAF Group Ltd* (1993) and *Star Rider Ltd* v *Inntrepreneur Pub Co* (1998). The position is unaffected by the Unfair Terms in Consumer Contracts Regulations 1994 which do not apply to businesses dealing with other businesses;

- *In extreme cases of disrepair*, the tenant may seek to rely on the court's power to order the appointment of a receiver and manager of the premises. Under s37 of the Supreme Court Act 1981, the High Court has power to appoint a receiver in all cases where it appears just and convenient so to do. A receiver has, accordingly, been appointed in cases where the landlord was in serious breach of his covenant to repair: see eg *Hart* v *Emelkirk Ltd* (1983), involving a block of flats.

Chapter 4

Assignment and Subletting

4.1 Introduction

In a formal lease, it is common to find an express covenant imposed by the landlord which seeks to restrict the tenant's ability to alienate (ie assign, sublet, charge, or part with possession of) the demised premises. Most commonly, the lease will permit assignment, subletting etc with the landlord's consent, such consent not to be unreasonably withheld. A vast body of case law has arisen on the question of when (ie in what circumstances) it is reasonable for the landlord to refuse or withhold his consent. The issue is now also governed by statute, in particular, the Landlord and Tenant Act 1988.

4.2 When can the tenant assign, sublet?

When can the tenant assign his lease or sublet the demised premises? The answer to this question will depend essentially on the terms of the lease. There are five possible situations:

- *The lease contains no restriction.* If this is so, the tenant can freely assign or sublet without obtaining consent from the landlord. Moreover, if the tenant agrees to take a lease which is to contain 'all the usual covenants', this will not entitle the landlord to the inclusion of a restriction on assignment in the lease;
- *The lease contains an absolute covenant* against assigning, subletting, parting with possession, charging etc of the demised premises. A simple prohibition, unqualified by any words requiring the consent of the landlord, entitles the landlord to withhold his consent in all circumstances and to impose what conditions he likes. By way of statutory exception, however, a covenant purporting to restrict prospective assignees or sub-lessees on grounds of colour, race, ethnic or national grounds, or sex is unlawful: see s24 of the Race Relations Act 1976 and s31 of the Sex Discrimination Act 1975;
- *The lease contains a qualified covenant.* A covenant not to assign, sublet, etc without obtaining the consent of the landlord

brings into operation s19(1) of the Landlord and Tenant Act 1927, which provides that, notwithstanding any provision to the contrary, such covenant shall be deemed to be subject to the proviso that such consent shall not be unreasonably withheld. The section does not absolve the tenant from the formality of seeking consent so that, if he goes ahead without seeking consent, he commits a breach regardless of the reasonableness of the transaction;

- *The lease contains an express proviso* that consent shall not be unreasonably withheld. Here, the parties have already predicted the effect of s19(1) and have included the additional words 'such consent not to be unreasonably withheld' in the covenant. The tenant is, therefore, in the same position as above;
- *The lease contains a covenant by the tenant* to offer a surrender of the lease to the landlord before assigning or subletting. Such a covenant is not invalidated by s19(1), but a clause requiring the tenant to offer a surrender of the lease before assignment will be void when contained in a business tenancy, since such a clause is contrary to s38(1) of the Landlord and Tenant Act 1954: *Allnatt London Properties Ltd* v *Newton* (1984).

A consent to an assignment, subletting, etc, given 'subject to licence' is, nevertheless, a binding and complete consent: *Prudential Assurance Co Ltd* v *Mount Eden Land Ltd* (1997) and *Next* v *National Farmers' Union Mutual Insurance Co* (1997). Similarly, a letter confirming that the landlord 'consents in principle' to a proposed transaction will almost certainly amount to a concluded consent.

4.3 What amounts to unreasonable withholding of consent?

4.3.1 *The Landlord and Tenant Act 1988*

Section 1 of the Landlord and Tenant Act 1988 imposes a duty on the landlord to consent to a tenant's application to assign, sublet, charge or part with possession of the demised premises, unless he has good reason for not doing so. Section 1(3) of the Act provides that, where the tenant serves a written application for consent to the transaction, the landlord owes a duty within a reasonable time:

- To give consent (except in a case where it is reasonable not to give consent);
- To serve on the tenant *written* notice of his decision whether or

not to give consent. If the consent is given subject to conditions, the landlord is also obliged to specify the conditions in his written notice. If the consent is withheld, the landlord must also state the reasons for withholding it.

Section 1(4) makes it clear that giving consent subject to an unreasonable condition does not satisfy the landlord's duty under s1(3) to give consent. Section 1(6) provides that the onus is on the landlord to show that:

- he gave consent within a reasonable time;
- his conditions (if any) are reasonable;
- his refusal of consent was reasonable; and
- he served written notice on the tenant within a reasonable time.

Section 2 of the Act places a further duty on the landlord to take reasonable steps to pass on the tenant's written application for consent to anyone he believes may be required to consent to the transaction. Thus, for example, a landlord who receives an application from a tenant, which also requires the consent of the superior landlord, is under a duty to send a copy of the application to the superior landlord.

Section 3 of the 1988 Act applies where a mesne tenant has covenanted not to consent to a disposition by his subtenant, without first obtaining approval to so doing from his own (superior) landlord. The provisions of s19(1) of the Landlord and Tenant Act 1927 (see 4.2 above) do not apply to such covenants. Section 3, therefore, will apply only where the covenant *expressly* states that the superior landlord may not unreasonably withhold consent. In such a case, s3 imposes a duty on the superior landlord, owed to both the mesne tenant and subtenant, not unreasonably to withhold consent. The mechanism for doing this mirrors that contained in s1 of the 1988 Act.

Whilst the 1988 Act reverses the burden of proof so that it is now necessary for the landlord to prove that any refusal is reasonable and provides the tenant with an action for damages for breach of statutory duty (see below), it does not alter the law in any other respect: *Air India* v *Balabel* (1993).

As mentioned above, the onus is on the landlord to show reasonable grounds for any delay in communicating his decision whether or not to give consent to a proposed assignment or subletting etc In *Midland Bank plc* v *Chart Enterprises Inc* (1990), the plaintiff bank sought consent from the defendant landlords to the assignment of their lease to a firm of solicitors. The bank's application to the landlords for consent was made by letter on 15 February 1989. After an initial acknowledgment, nothing significant occurred from the landlord's side in the way of correspondence until 5 May 1989. The landlord's letter of 5 May 1989 was interpreted by the Court as a consent subject to conditions, at least one of which was totally unacceptable. The delay was by this time clearly unreasonable, but some months of further delay occurred. Some time was occupied by a query as to the kind of tenancy held by the occupant of the flat on the second and third floors of the premises and whether he was an employee of the bank, a matter which the landlords could have checked by an inquiry to their predecessors in title. Correspondence continued until July 1989 and eventually, in August 1989, the bank issued proceedings seeking a declaration that the landlords had unreasonably delayed in communicating their decision whether or not to grant consent to the proposed assignment. The landlords argued that they were entitled, when approached for consent, to take some time in making enquiries if they have a suspicion that there might have been a breach of covenant as to subletting. The Court, however, rejected this argument. Applying s1(6) of the 1988 Act, the landlords had not shown that they had reasonable grounds for the delay. Similarly, in *Dong Bang Minerva (UK) Ltd* v *Davina Ltd* (1995), the tenant's request to sublet part of the property described the proposed transaction sufficiently for the landlord's purposes and any legitimate concern which the landlord might have had about the terms of the sublease could have been adequately met by means of a condition that it must approve the final form of the sublease. The landlord was in a position to give (and ought reasonably to have given) such conditional consent by 8 August 1993 at the latest and, since it had not done so, it was held to be in breach of its statutory duty under the 1988 Act.

It is now clear that a landlord can only rely on reasons for withholding consent which are stated in writing within a reasonable time of the tenant's application for consent. In *Footwear Corporation Ltd* v *Amplight Properties Ltd* (1998), the tenant of retail premises wrote to the landlord seeking consent to a subletting. Three days later, the landlord's managing director telephoned the tenant's surveyor indicating that consent would not be granted for a variety of reasons. The Court held that the landlord was not entitled to rely on reasons justifying its refusal which had not been communicated to the tenant in *writing* within a reasonable time in compliance with s1(3) of the Act. The upshot of this decision, therefore, is that:

- If the landlord gives *no* reasons within a reasonable time of the tenant's application for consent, he cannot rely in court on *any* reasons which, in fact, brought about that refusal;
- If the landlord has given *written* reasons for refusal within a reasonable time, he cannot rely on *unstated* reasons which may also have affected his decision to refuse consent; and
- If the landlord has given *verbal* reasons within a reasonable time, he cannot rely on these (or any other) reasons for justifying refusal of consent.

4.3.2 General considerations

It is, in each case, a question of fact, depending on all the circumstances, whether the landlord's consent to an assignment or subletting is being unreasonably withheld. Thus, for example, it is reasonable for a landlord to refuse his consent to an assignment of the lease where the proposed assignee would, unlike the assignor, become entitled to purchase the freehold under the Leasehold Reform Act 1967: *Norfolk Capital Group Ltd* v *Kitway Ltd* (1977) and *Bickel* v *Duke of Westminster* (1977).

The landlord's withholding of consent will be justified if a reasonable man in the landlord's position might have regarded the proposed transaction as damaging to his property interests, even though some persons might take a different view. Thus, in *Re Town Investments Ltd Underlease* (1954), the tenant proposed to sublet the premises at a large premium and reduced rent. The landlord objected on the ground that the low rent might prejudice future dealings with the property. The Court held that these fears could not be said to be unfounded. By contrast, in *Parker* v *Boggon* (1947), the landlord feared that the proposed assignee, a diplomat, might invoke diplomatic privilege. The Court held that these fears were exaggerated.

A landlord's refusal to consent to an assignment will be unreasonable if it is designed to achieve a collateral result unconnected with the terms of the lease or the parties, even though the purpose is in accordance with good estate management. In *Bromley Park Garden Estates Ltd* v *Moss* (1982), the landlords were the owners of a two-storey building, the ground floor of which was let to A and used as a restaurant and the first floor of which was let to B and used as a residential flat. The lease of the flat contained a covenant that it was not to be assigned without the landlord's consent. In 1980, B wished to assign the lease to the defendant and applied to the landlords for their consent to the assignment. The landlords refused stating that it was not their policy to permit assignments of residential tenancies and that if B wished to vacate the flat she would be required to surrender the lease. B, nevertheless, went ahead and assigned the lease to the defendant. The landlords then issued proceedings claiming possession of the flat alleging a breach of the covenant in the lease restricting assignment. The defendant contended that the covenant was subject (by virtue of s19(1) of the Landlord and Tenant Act 1927) to a proviso that the landlords' consent was not to be unreasonably withheld and that the landlords had withheld their consent unreasonably. The landlords' agent stated in evidence that, in the interests of the proper management of their estate, the landlords' policy was where possible not to permit multiple lettings in the same premises because it lowered their investment value. The agent also stated that A(the ground floor tenant) had in the past expressed an interest in taking a lease of the whole building. The Court of Appeal held that, since the landlords' reason for refusing consent (namely, that a single lease of the whole building would enhance its investment value) was wholly extraneous to, and unconnected with, the bargain made by the parties to the lease when the covenant was granted, their refusal of consent was unreasonable.

Where a proposed assignment would on paper cause a detriment to the landlord's reversion but, in the actual circumstances of the case, that detriment would not arise, a refusal of consent by the landlord is unreasonable. In *International Drilling Fluids Ltd* v *Louisville Investments (Uxbridge) Ltd* (1986), the lease provided that the property was not to be used 'for any purpose other than offices' and that the tenant was not to assign the premises without the consent of the landlord which was 'not to be unreasonably withheld'. The lease was assigned to the tenants, who entered into a covenant with the landlords to pay the rent. Later, the tenants vacated the premises and sought the landlords' consent to assign the lease. The landlords refused on the grounds that the proposed use of the premises as service offices would be detrimental to the investment value of the reversion. The Court of Appeal, however, held that, although the landlord usually needed to consider his own relevant interests, it was unreasonable for him to refuse consent if the detriment to the tenant was extreme and disproportionate to its benefit to the landlord. Where, therefore, the proposed user was within the only specific type of use permitted by the lease, it was unreasonable to refuse consent to the assignment on the ground of that user when the landlord was fully secured for the payment of rent and the result of the refusal was that the property would be left vacant. Moreover, since there was no prospect of the landlord actually realising the reversion by mortgaging or selling the property during the remainder of the lease, the disadvantage which the landlord would suffer by diminution in value of what was in effect merely the paper value of the reversion was minimal and, therefore, disproportionate to the harm which would be suffered by the tenant (who had already vacated the building but remained liable for the performance of the tenant's obligations under the lease) if the landlord refused consent. Since the landlord ought to have considered the detriment to the tenant, his refusal of consent was also unreasonable on this alternative ground.

The decision in *International Drilling Fluids* (above) may be contrasted with *Ponderosa International Development Inc v Pengap Securities (Bristol) Ltd* (1986), where the landlords considered that the financial standing of the proposed assignees and their guarantors was insufficient, not only because of its intrinsic inadequacy but also because the proposed assignment would mean the substitution of a less attractive tenant for that of a group with an international reputation. The tenants argued that, although the market might be influenced by this latter consideration, this attitude was unreasonable as by law the original tenants remained continuously liable upon the covenants, if called upon, despite the assignment. The *International Drilling Fluids* case differed from the instant case in at least two important respects. First, in the former, there was no prospect or need for the landlords to sell the reversion whereas, in the *Ponderosa* case, the landlords needed to sell. Secondly, in the *International Drilling Fluids* case there was a detriment to the tenants whereas, in *Ponderosa*, there was not, as the landlords were willing to consent to a subletting. Consequently, the very principles which in the *International Drilling Fluids* case led to the decision that the landlords had unreasonably refused their consent led in the *Ponderosa* case, subject to two questions, to the conclusion that the landlords had not unreasonably withheld it. The first question was whether the landlords were entitled to take into account the attitude of the market (mentioned above) despite the contingent liability of the original tenants after assignment. The Court held on this point that the landlords were so entitled as they lived in the real world and had to take the market as they found it, not as lawyers might wish it to be. The second question was whether the landlords were unreasonable in taking a less than favourable view of the financial standing of the proposed assignees and guarantors. On this point, the Court held that the landlords were not being unreasonable since the assignees' capitalisation and debt position and the references provided as to the guarantors' financial standing justified the landlords' reservations.

4.3.3 *Particular considerations*

Below is a list of particular considerations which the courts have considered in determining whether or not the landlord has unreasonably withheld consent to an assignment or subletting:

- *Refusal based on grounds of race, nationality or sex.* As mentioned earlier, refusal based on grounds of colour, race, ethnic or national origins, or sex is deemed to be unreasonable, except where the landlord shares part of the residential accommodation comprised in the tenancy: see s24(2) of the Race Relations Act 1976 and s31(2) of the Sex Discrimination Act 1975. Even where the landlord does share part of the accommodation, his refusal on such grounds may be unreasonable according to general principles;
- *Request for outstanding information.* A request for 'full details of the transaction' without specifying the issue of concern will not justify the landlord's refusal in giving a decision: *Norwich Union Life Insurance Society* v *Shopmoor Ltd* (1998);
- *Unreasonable conditions.* The imposition of unreasonable conditions amounts to unreasonable refusal of consent: s1(6) of the Landlord and Tenant Act 1988. Conditions designed to extort an advantage not otherwise obtainable are unreasonable. For, example, in *Premier Rinks* v *Amalgamated Cinematograph Theatres Ltd* (1912), the tenants desired to assign the lease, but the landlords refused consent except on condition of the insertion in the lease of a covenant not to use the demised premises for the purposes of a cinema. This was designed to prevent the tenants from competing with the landlords' cinema adjoining the demised premises. The Court held that the landlords were acting unreasonably in withholding consent to the assignment without the inclusion of the restrictive covenant, and were seeking to take advantage of the assignment to procure the insertion in the lease

of a restriction that was not originally there, which they were not entitled to do. Similarly, in *Young* v *Ashley Gardens Properties Ltd* (1903), the landlord unreasonably required the proposed assignee to assume a rates burden not contained in the lease. In *Orlando Investments Ltd* v *Grosvenor Estate Belgravia* (1989), the Court of Appeal held that it was not unreasonable, in the circumstances, for the landlord to require the proposed assignee to carry out essential works of repair to the premises and to provide security for the due execution of the work. This was required as evidence of the proposed assignee's willingness to do the repairs, not his financial ability to do them, and it was not unreasonable given the past history of breaches for the landlord to require proof of the proposed assignee's willingness to perform. It has been held that an offer to accept a surrender in lieu of the tenant assigning is not a reasonable ground for refusing consent: *Straudley Investments Ltd* v *Mount Eden Land Ltd* (1997);

- **Disrepair**. The mere fact that the tenant is committing a continuing breach of a covenant to repair does not necessarily entitle the landlord to refuse his consent to a proposed assignment: *Farr* v *Ginnings* (1928). For example, in *Straudley Investments Ltd* v *Mount Eden Land Ltd* (1997), an outstanding forfeiture notice relating to a non-urgent repair did not justify the landlord's refusal to deal with an application for consent. However, where the lack of repair is serious, the landlord's position is much stronger: *Goldstein* v *Saunders* (1915). In *Orlando Investments Ltd* v *Grosvenor Estate Belgravia* (1989), referred to above, the Court of Appeal held that, where there are extensive long-standing breaches of a covenant to repair, it is not unreasonable for the landlord to refuse his consent to an assignment unless he can be reasonably satisfied that the proposed assignee would remedy them. In this case, given the history of the case, and in particular that this was the second proposed assignment where no repairs had been done and that the proposed assignee had already shown himself disinclined to carry out essential remedial work, the landlord was not acting unreasonably in requiring the work to be done within a stated timetable. Nor was it unreasonable to require the proposed assignee to provide security for the due execution of the works. It was suggested in argument that it was not unreasonable for a landlord to withhold consent if he will have the same rights of enforcement of the repairing covenant against the assignee as he has against the assignor tenant. This was rejected by the Court on the basis that the landlord is entitled to be reasonably satisfied that the assignee will remedy the breaches as a precondition of granting consent;

- *Proposed assignee a limited company.* The landlord cannot reasonably refuse his consent on this ground: *Willmott v London Road Car Co Ltd* (1910) and in *Re Greater London Properties Ltd's Lease* (1959);

- *Outstanding rent review.* It will usually be unreasonable to link consent to the resolution of a rent review or a proposed variation of the terms of the lease: *Dong Bang Minerva (UK) Ltd v Davina Ltd* (1995);

- *Statutory protection.* The fact that the proposed assignee or subtenant would enjoy statutory protection not enjoyed by the tenant may be a reasonable ground for refusal, particularly if consent is being sought shortly before the expiry of the term. For example, in *Lee v K Carter Ltd* (1949), the landlord was held justified in refusing consent to an assignment by a tenant company of a flat to an individual director: see also *Swanson v Forton* (1949), where the tenant, who was out of possession and so incapable of enjoying a statutory tenancy under the Rent Acts, proposed to assign 12 days before expiry of the term; and *Re Cooper's Lease* (1968) where the proposed subtenant would acquire statutory protection under Part II of the Landlord and Tenant Act 1954. These decisions may be contrasted with *Thomas Bookman Ltd v Nathan* (1955), where seven and a half months remained unexpired and the object of the assignment had nothing to do with acquiring protection under the Rent Acts;

- *Breach of user covenant.* Refusal of consent may be reasonable if the proposed assignment will result in breach of user covenants. However, in most cases, breach of a user covenant is not a necessary consequence of assigning or subletting. In *Killick v Second Covent Garden Property Co* (1973), a user covenant in the lease prohibited the tenant from using the premises 'for any other purpose than the trade or business of a printer... without the [landlords'] written consent which shall not be unreasonably withheld'. The tenant wished to assign the lease to a company which proposed to use the premises as offices. The landlords refused their consent to the assignment on the ground that a breach of user covenant would be a necessary consequence of the assignment. The Court of Appeal, however, disagreed, holding that even if the user covenant precluded the assignee from using the premises as offices, it was not a necessry consequence of the assignment that there would be a breach as, once the assignment had been made, the landlords would have the same rights to enforce the user covenant against the assignee as they had against the tenant. Moreover, on the true construction of the user covenant, the words 'without the [landlords'] written consent which shall not be unreasonably withheld' meant that the landlords could not object to any reasonable user of the premises. Thus, the assignment did not (in any event) necessarily involve a breach of covenant. For these reasons, the landlords' refusal of consent was held to be unreasonable.

In *British Bakeries (Midlands) Ltd* v *Michael Testler & Co Ltd* (1986), the landlord refused consent on the ground of the proposed user of the premises. This ground was rejected by the Court in the light of the *Killick* decision (mentioned above) as being merely an expectation of a future breach of user covenant, which did not provide a good reason for a refusal of consent. The *Killick* case, however, distinguished in *FW Woolworth plc* v *Charlwood Alliance Properties Ltd* (1986) on the ground that, in the former case, the user covenant was positive in nature and, therefore, capable of enforcement by prohibitory injunction, whilst in the latter case the covenant was negative in terms. Moreover, in the latter case, the breach had already taken place and the proposed assignees had no intention of observing the user clause so that consent to the assignment would inevitably involve the landlord in waiving his rights to object to the existing breach;

- **The landlord's letting policy.** In *Moss Bros Group plc* v *CSC Properties Ltd* (1999), the landlord was held to have reasonably withheld consent to an assignment of a lease of a men's fashion store in a major shopping mall to an electronic games retailer on the ground that the assignment and change of use would conflict with its policy of reserving that part of the mall for fashion-related stores. Given such a tenant-mix policy, it was not unreasonable to conclude that the games retailer would attract a clientele that was, for the most part, quite different from the shoppers who would seek out the fashion-related stores;

- **The landlord requires possession for himself.** The landlord cannot reasonably refuse his consent simply because he desires to obtain possession of the premises for his own use: *Bates* v *Donaldson* (1896);

- **The landlord's business interests.** A genuine fear by the landlord that his business interests in the reversion will suffer is a reasonable ground for withholding of consent: *Pimms Ltd* v

Tallow Chandlers Co (1964), where there was a danger that the proposed assignee would be strongly placed to compel the landlord to agree to his participation in the landlord's scheme for redeveloping the area; *Premier Confectionery (London) Co Ltd* v *London Commercial Sale Rooms Ltd* (1933), where occupation of two shops by separate tenants was considered detrimental to the landlord's property; and *Sportoffer Ltd* v *Erewash Borough Council* (1999), where the landlord had a reasonable fear that the tenant's proposed change of user would involve a real threat of competition to his adjoining business interests;

- *The financial standing of the proposed assignee.* This will be of primary importance to the landlord in deciding whether or not to consent to the proposed assignment. Apart from the usual references provided by banks, solicitors, accountants etc, the landlord may be entitled to ask for the trading profits of the proposed assignee with a view to satisfying himself of the latter's capability of meeting his obligations under the lease. In *British Bakeries (Midlands) Ltd* v *Michael Testler & Co* (1986), the landlord refused consent to a proposed assignment on the ground, *inter alia*, of the financial ability of the proposed assignees. The tenants put forward six sets of references as to the assignees' financial ability from accountants, bankers, solicitors, accountants, estate agents and two trade references, and also submitted accounts relating to the assignees' past trading. The references, however, related to the assignees' previous business and premises, whereas they were intending to embark upon a further venture in premises with a higher rent. A number of the property valuations were unreliable and the audited accounts were not such as to remove a reasonable landlord's doubts as to the proposed assignees' financial liability. Not surprisingly, it was held that the landlord was not acting unreasonably in refusing consent in view of his real doubts as to the assignees' ability to meet the obligations under the lease. In *Warren* v *Marketing Exchange for Africa Ltd* (1988), the Court confirmed that a landlord need not be content with references of a qualified and superficial nature.

The trading accounts of the proposed assignee are likely to be a better guide to the proposed assignees' financial ability than references. The accounts will show the capital adequacy of the assignee and the general level of profitability. The best indicator of whether the assignee will be able to pay the rent is the profit and loss account. In the *British Bakeries* case, referred to above, evidence was given that 'a generally accepted test of the financial standing of any proposed assignee is that his accounts should show a pre-tax profit of not less than three-times the amount payable under the lease'. (The pre-tax profit is the relevant figure because it is that profit against which the rent will be charged). This test, however, is only a guide. In *Venetian Glass Gallery Ltd v Next Properties Ltd* (1989), the proposed assignee was a limited company whose recent trading profits were poor, but it was improving its trade and other factors (eg the availability of a strong guarantee) showed that the company was suitable despite its low profit margin.

Another aspect of the accounts which may be relevant is the balance sheet since this will show the net asset value of the assignee, which may be relevant in so far as the landlord may have to sue for rent and rely on a suitable asset base from which to recover its debt;

- *The requirement of a surety.* Generally speaking, a surety or guarantor may be reasonably required by the landlord as a condition of granting consent to a proposed assignment if the assignee is of insufficient financial standing but, ultimately, much will depend on the particular circumstances of the case: in *Re Greater London Properties Ltd's Lease* (1959). Many commercial leases will contain a covenant stating that sureties may be required by the landlord on an assignment of the lease. It seems that such an express requirement will be enforceable despite s19(1) of the Landlord and Tenant Act 1927: *Vaux Group plc v Lilley* (1991). In other words, the section will not have the effect of relieving the tenant from his express obligation of obtaining, if the landlord so requires, an acceptable guarantor upon an assignment of the lease;

- *The taking of a fine.* Under s144 of the Law of Property Act 1925, every covenant against assigning, subletting etc without the landlord's consent shall, unless the contrary is expressed, be deemed to be subject to a proviso that no sum of money in the nature of a fine shall be payable for such consent. The landlord may, however, require the payment of a reasonable sum in respect of legal or other expenses incurred in granting such consent: s19(1)(a) of the Landlord and Tenant Act 1927: see *Dong Bang Minerva (UK) Ltd v Davina Ltd* (1995), where the landlords were held to have acted unreasonably in relation to the form and nature of the undertaking as to costs by requiring the tenants to be 'fully' responsible for 'all' their costs, as opposed to their reasonable costs. There is some uncertainty as to whether a rental deposit constitutes a 'fine' for the purposes of s144. It has been held, in a different context, that a large sum paid at the commencement of a lease and purporting to represent rent paid in advance was a fine for the purpose of deciding whether a lease was at a rent or a premium: *Hughes* v *Waite* (1957). That decision is, however, distinguishable on the basis that the word 'fine' in *Hughes* was being used to describe a single capital payment as opposed to recurrent income payments by way of rent, whereas in s144 the word is used to denote a sum in the nature of a penalty. The decision in *Re Cosh's Contract* (1897) also points to the conclusion that, for the purpose of s144, a deposit by way of a security is not a fine. The point, however, remains an open one. Although a rental deposit may not be a fine prohibited by s144, it does not mean that a deposit may be demanded by the landlord as a matter of course. The demand must still, in the case of a qualified covenant, have to satisfy the requirement of reasonableness.

4.4 Authorised guarantee agreements

The Landlord and Tenant (Covenants) Act 1995 introduced a new regime of landlord and tenant covenant liability into leases granted on or after 1 January 1996. It also modified existing leases from that date by introducing procedures to assist former tenants with continuing leasehold liability. (This is discussed fully in Ch 6, at 6.2). In the present context, it is important to note that the 1995 Act has amended s19 of the Landlord and Tenant Act 1927 in a number of significant respects.

Under a lease granted after 1 January 1996, a former tenant will remain liable for the defaults of his immediate assignee if the landlord obtains an 'authorised guarantee agreement' from him guaranteeing performance of the tenant's covenants by his immediate assignee. The landlord may require such an agreement from the former tenant either (a) automatically as one of the conditions for assignment set out in the covenant in the lease, or (b) otherwise because it is reasonable to do so.

As to (a), the parties to a new lease are given the right (under the 1995 Act) to agree in advance the conditions which the former tenant or prospective assignee must meet as a precondition of the landlord's consent to the assignment. Examples of typical conditions will include: the assignee must have net profits before tax in its most recent accounts of at least three-times the rent; the assignee must provide a rent deposit or guarantor; the former tenant must enter into an authorised guarantee agreement. So far as the latter is concerned, any form of commercial guarantee is permissible, so long as no term of the guarantee prevents the former tenant's statutory right to be released from the guarantee upon a further assignment by his immediate assignee. (To the extent that the former tenant is not so released, the agreement is not an authorised guarantee agreement and is void under the 1995 Act's anti-avoidance provisions).

As to (b), this will apply where the landlord's consent is required to the assignment and the landlord gives that consent on condition that the former tenant enters into an authorised guarantee agreement. The condition must be lawfully imposed, and so this situation will arise in either of two cases: (a) where the lease contains an absolute prohibition against assignment, but the landlord decides in his discretion to permit the assignment if the former tenant offers a guarantee; or (b) (more commonly) where the lease requires the landlord's consent which cannot be unreasonably withheld (whether as a result of s19(1) of the 1927 Act or because of an express proviso to that effect) and it is reasonable for the landlord to require a guarantee from the former tenant as a condition of granting his consent. Whether it is reasonable for the landlord to insist on an authorised guarantee as a precondition of granting consent will depend on all the circumstances of the case.

4.5 What acts by the tenant constitute a breach?

4.5.1 *Covenant construed against the landlord*

The covenant not to assign, sublet etc will be construed *contra proferentem* (ie against the landlord in whose favour it is included into the lease). Thus, the subletting of part of the demised premises is not a breach unless the covenant extends to 'the demised premises or *any part thereof*'. The position will be different if the tenant, having sublet part, sublets the rest.

The taking in of lodgers, paying guests or permitting licensees to use the premises is not a breach of the covenant not to part with *possession* (as opposed to occupation): *Stening v Abrahams* (1931), where the Court held that such a covenant was not broken by the grant of a seven-year exclusive licence to erect an advertisement hoarding against the front wall of the tenant's house. A licence, of course, merely constitutes a permission to occupy without affording the occupier exclusive possession of the premises.

4.5.2 *Must be a voluntary disposition inter-vivos*

The covenant is not broken by:

- the vesting of the lease in the tenant's trustee in bankruptcy;
- the mortgage of the demised property by way of charge (as opposed to sub-demise);
- the compulsory purchase of the demised premises; and
- a bequest of the leasehold interest by will.

4.6 Landlord's remedies for breach

The landlord's remedies for breach of the tenant's covenant against assignment, subletting, charging, parting with possession etc are as follows:

- *Damages.* This will invariably be the least useful remedy since it will leave the assignee in occupation of the demised premises. As to the measure of damages, see *Williams* v *Earle* (1868);
- *Forfeiture of the lease.* It is important to note that the assignment or subletting is not *void* but *voidable* at the option of the landlord. In other words, the assignee (or subtenant) will take a defeasible title (ie subject to the landlord's right of forfeiture). If the assignee (or subtenant) is in possession, he should be made a defendant and possession claimed against him. Because the assignment is an effective assignment and only voidable (at the election of the landlord), it is the assignee who will be concerned to avoid a forfeiture and not the original tenant.

  The fact that a breach of the covenant has been committed through forgetfulness or because the tenant thought it unimportant will not form a ground for giving him equitable relief against forfeiture: *Eastern Telegraph Co Ltd* v *Dent* (1899);
- *Injunction.* This is an important remedy where the tenant threatens to assign or sublet in breach of covenant. It is also a useful remedy to enforce a covenant against subletting: *Hemingway Securities Ltd* v *Dunraven Ltd* (1995), where a mandatory injunction was obtained against the subtenant requiring him to execute a deed delivering up its unlawful sublease to the tenant.

4.7 Tenant's remedies where consent unreasonably withheld

If the tenant has gone ahead with the transaction, he can simply

wait for the landlord to sue and then set up the unrea
refusal by way of defence, and counterclaim for a declaration   at
the landlord's refusal was unreasonable and that the tenant was
entitled, notwithstanding the refusal, to assign or sublet.

Alternatively, where the tenant does not want to take the risk of
going ahead and assigning etc without consent, he may apply to
the County Court for a declaration that the consent has been
unreasonably withheld. This jurisdiction is given by s53 of the
Landlord and Tenant Act 1954. Additionally to the foregoing, the
tenant may bring an action for damages alleging that the landlord
is in breach of his statutory duty under s1(3) of the Landlord and
Tenant Act 1988. The right to claim such damages is conferred by s4
of the 1988 Act. Because a breach of this statutory duty gives rise to
damages in tort, the tenant is entitled to be put in the position he
would have been if the tort had not been committed; damages will,
therefore, include all those losses which were reasonably foreseeable at the time when the tort was committed. An action for
damages may be combined with a claim for an injunction requiring
the landlord to comply with his statutory duty.

Chapter 5

Other Covenants

5.1 Introduction

Apart from the covenant to pay rent, to repair, and not to assign, sublet, etc there are also a number of other covenants which will be contained in the lease. In the absence of an express covenant dealing with the point, the law will automatically imply certain covenants into the lease on the part of the landlord and tenant. The most important implied covenants on the part of the landlord concern quiet enjoyment, non-derogation from grant (discussed in 5.2 and 5.3) and liability to repair the demised premises (discussed in 3.7). There are also a number of covenants implied by law on the part of the tenant. These include the obligation to pay rent (discussed in 2.1), not to commit waste and use the premises in a tenant-like manner (discussed briefly in 3.8).

5.2 Quiet enjoyment

Most formally drafted leases will contain an express covenant on the part of the landlord that the tenant is entitled to quiet enjoyment of the demised premises. In the absence of express provision, a covenant for quiet enjoyment will be automatically implied by law.

As its name suggests, this covenant is designed to ensure that the tenant may peacefully enjoy the demised property without interruption from the landlord or persons claiming under him (eg other tenants in the same building). Most commonly, a breach of the covenant arises when the landlord seeks forcibly to evict the tenant from the premises. In such circumstances, exemplary damages may be awarded for the unlawful eviction where the facts constitute the tort of trespass or nuisance: *Drane* v *Evangelou* (1978) (removal of belongings and change of locks), and *Guppy's (Bridport) Ltd* v *Brookling* (1984) (two tenants forced to leave their rooms due to the extent of disruption caused by the landlord's building works). Exemplary damages are awarded not to compensate the tenant for any loss he may have suffered as a consequence of the unlawful eviction, but simply to 'teach the landlord a lesson'. In addition to claiming exemplary damages, the tenant may seek compensation for any damage to (or loss of) his goods and the cost of alternative premises while wrongfully kept out of the demised property. Damages may also be awarded to compensate for inconvenience and discomfort but not, it seems, for injured feelings and mental distress: *Branchett* v *Beaney* (1992).

A landlord will also be liable under the covenant if he causes physical interference with the tenant's land, irrespective of whether he has actually intruded onto the demised premises: *Kenny* v *Preen* (1963). In *Owen* v *Gadd* (1956), the landlords let a shop to the tenants, reserving to themselves the floor above the shop. Three days after the grant of the lease, contractors, instructed by the landlords, erected on the pavement in front of the shop scaffolding for the purpose of carrying out repairs to the landlords' upper premises. Access to the tenant's shop window was partially obstructed by the scaffolding. The landlords did what they could to minimise the damage and the repairs were completed and the scaffolding removed within two weeks. The Court of Appeal held that there could be a breach of the covenant for quiet enjoyment without an actual physical interruption into or upon the demised premises. The scaffold poles constituted a substantial interruption and the tenants were, accordingly, entitled to damages for breach of the covenant. On the same basis, the landlord's act of cutting off the tenant's gas and electricity supply to the premises from outside will constitute a breach even in the absence of any direct physical interference with the premises: *Perera* v *Vandiyar* (1953). The covenant also includes an obligation on the part of the landlord to allow the tenant into possession of the demised property so that, in the event that a previous tenant wrongfully remains in occupation, with the landlord's acquiescence, the new (incoming) tenant may sue the landlord for breach of the covenant: *Miller* v *Emcer Products Ltd* (1956). It seems that an omission on the part of the landlord which is a breach of duty (eg to repair) may constitute a breach of the covenant for quiet enjoyment: *Hafton Properties Ltd* v *Camp* (1993).

It has recently been held that, where tenants of the same landlord are adjoining occupiers, and one tenant's reasonable use and enjoyment of his premises is interfered with by noise from the ordinary use of the adjoining property, their landlord is not liable either for breach of covenant for quiet enjoyment or in nuisance: *Southwark London Borough Council* v *Mills* (1998) and *Baxter* v *Camden London Borough Council (No 2)* (1999). Thus, a mere interference with the comfort of the tenant using the demised premises by the creation of a personal annoyance (eg from noise, invasion of privacy, etc) is not sufficient to constitute a breach of the covenant. In *Jenkins v Jackson* (1888), for example, a room above the demised premises was let for dancing and other entertainments. It was held that the annoyance from the dancing, although a nuisance, did not constitute a breach.

The covenant for quiet enjoyment does not normally extend to interruptions committed by the owner of a superior title to that of the landlord. In other words, the covenant only extends to the acts of the landlord and those claiming through or under him. Only an absolute covenant for quiet enjoyment will extend to interruptions by persons claiming under title paramount. A good illustration of this principle is to be found in the case of *Kelly v Rodgers* (1892). Here, the superior landlord brought forfeiture proceedings against the sublessor and recovered possession of the premises for non-payment of rent. The Court of Appeal held that there was no breach of the covenant for quiet enjoyment because the interruption was that of a person claiming under title paramount (as opposed to that of the sublessor or any person claiming by, through, or under him). The position will be different, however, if the sublessor has consented to judgment for possession against him by a superior landlord and this is the cause of the tenant's interruption. The point was addressed in *Cohen v Tanner* (1900), where the superior landlord brought an action against the sublessor to recover possession of the premises for breach of a covenant against assignment. The sublessor gave the tenant notice of the action, telling him that there was no defence, and signed a consent to judgment for possession, under which the tenant was evicted. The Court of Appeal, distinguishing the case of *Kelly*, held that, as the sublessor had a good defence to the action, his act in consenting to judgment was the cause of the interruption of the tenant's enjoyment and was, therefore, a breach of the covenant for quiet enjoyment. The general rule, therefore, is that the covenant for quiet enjoyment does not include any promise by the sublessor that he will not lessen his title by the act (eg forfeiture) of the superior landlord. In order to constitute a breach of the covenant, there has to be something more than the mere act of the superior landlord. In *Cohen*, the sublessor had actively 'given' the superior landlord the right to evict the tenant, Since this was the effective cause of the tenant being turned out, there was a clear breach of the covenant.

The covenant extends to all *lawful* and *unlawful* acts of

interference by the landlord. This, however, does not include acts committed pursuant to the lease itself, for example, a landlord's re-entry for breach of a tenant's covenant. Nor is the landlord liable under the covenant for a nuisance caused by another of his tenants because he knows the latter is causing the nuisance and does not himself take any steps to prevent what is being done. In order to render the landlord liable in such circumstances, there must be active participation on his part or a sufficiently positive act amounting to authorisation of the nuisance: *Malzy* v *Eicholz* (1916).

It is important to stress that the covenant only extends to the *lawful* acts of persons claiming under the landlord (eg other tenants). In *Sanderson* v *The Mayor of Berwick-on-Tweed Corporation* (1884), the defendant landlords let farmland to three separate tenants, T1, T2 and T3. T1 suffered damage as a result of the flooding of drains situate on the demised land of T2 and T3. It was held that the landlords were liable only for the damage to T1's land resulting from T3's proper use of drains which were defective, but not for T2's excessive (and, hence, unlawful) use of drains which were in good order. In *Queensway Marketing Ltd* v *Associated Restaurants Ltd* (1988), the Court drew a distinction between an express covenant against interruptions by any person or persons claiming through or under the landlord and an express covenant against interruptions by a *named* person. In the former case, the landlord is liable only if the interruption is lawful but, in the latter case, he is liable whether the interruption is lawful or unlawful. In the instant case, a named person was not identified in the covenant but the expression 'superior lessors' was an identification by reference to a particular interest in property (ie the superior lessors or their successors in title). Accordingly, the Court of Appeal held that the landlords were liable for the acts of their superior lessors which constituted an interruption of the tenant's enjoyment of the premises, whether the acts were lawful or unlawful.

There are several statutory provisions which make it a criminal offence for a landlord to unlawfully evict or harass a residential tenant: s1 of the Protection from Eviction Act 1977. Section 27(3) of the Housing Act 1988 also imposes a statutory liability to pay damages on a landlord who personally, or through his agents, has committed acts which amount to the offences of unlawful eviction or harassment under the 1977 Act. These provisions do not apply to commercial lettings.

5.3 Non-derogation from grant

A landlord is subject to an implied covenant not to derogate from his grant. Essentially, if a landlord lets land for a particular purpose, he must not do anything which prevents it being used for that purpose. The covenant differs from quiet enjoyment in *three* important respects:

- Non-derogation only operates when the landlord lets part of his land and retains the other part – the covenant limits the use that can be made of the retained part;
- If the tenant intends to use the premises for some special use, this must be made known to the landlord at the commencement of the letting in order to render the latter liable under the covenant. For example, in *Robinson* v *Kilvert* (1889), the tenant used the demised premises for the storage of paper which was peculiarly susceptible to heat. This was not made known to the landlord at the time of the letting, who commenced a manufacture in the cellar below involving a heating apparatus which damaged the paper. The Court of Appeal held that the landlord had not derogated from grant;
- The tenant need only show that the landlord has rendered the demised premises less fit for the purpose for which they were let. In *Harmer* v *Jumbil (Nigeria) Tin Areas Ltd* (1921), the premises were let for the purpose of storing explosives. The landlords wished to use the adjoining land for mining, which would jeopordise the tenant's licence to store explosives under the Explosives Act 1875. It was held that this constituted a derogation from grant.

It is not sufficient for the tenant merely to show that the landlord has inconvenienced him, his privacy or amenity, but rather that the interference is of such a serious nature as to frustrate the use of the premises for the purpose for which they were demised: *Browne* v *Flower* (1911) (mere interference with privacy insufficient). In *Kelly* v *Battershell* (1949), the Court of Appeal held, applying the *Browne* case, that the incorporation of the subject building into an adjoining hotel did not amount to a derogation from grant, since the increased user was merely an interference with the tenant's convenience, amenity or privacy and was not of such a serious nature as to frustrate the use of the tenant's premises for the purpose for which they were demised (ie that of a private residence).

In *Port* v *Griffith* (1938), the landlords let a shop to the tenant, the latter covenanting to use and occupy the premises for the sale of wool and general trimmings. Some six years later, the landlords let the adjoining shop subject to a similar covenant, the business stated being for the sale of tailor and dressmaking trimmings and cloths. The tenant argued that this was a derogation from grant as frustrating the purpose for which the premises were let to him. The Court held that it was not within the contemplation of the parties that the landlords were putting themselves under an obligation not to let their adjoining property to the tenant's trade rival. The case was followed in *Romulus Trading Co Ltd* v *Comet Properties Ltd* (1996), where the demised premises were used for the business of banking. The landlords let nearby premises to another tenant for a similar use. The Court reiterated the view that, if premises were let for a particular trade, there was nothing to prevent the landlord from leasing an adjoining property for the same purpose.

5.4 Alterations and improvements

A commercial lease will invariably contain an express covenant whereby the tenant agrees not to alter or improve the demised premises. Such a covenant may amount to an absolute restriction on the tenant's ability to alter or improve the property or may be qualified in that only such alterations or improvements as are authorised by the landlord may be carried out.

5.4.1 Alterations

An alteration involves a change in the form, constitution or fabric of a building. Examples of such changes include the conversion of a house into flats: *Duke of Westminster* v *Swinton* (1948). But the change must necessarily involve something more than just a change to the appearance of the building. Clear examples of alterations include the conversion of two rooms into one, the subdivision of rooms, the creation and moving of existing doorways and windows, or the demolition of attached outhouses.

Aqualified covenant against alterations is subject to a proviso that the landlord's licence or consent to the making of improvements is not to be unreasonably withheld: s19(2) of the Landlord and Tenant Act 1927. The proviso does not preclude the landlord's right to require, as a condition of such licence or consent, the payment of a reasonable sum in respect of any damage to or diminution in the value of the premises (or any neighbouring premises) belonging to the landlord, and of any legal or other expenses properly incurred in connection with such licence or consent. In the case of an improvement which does not add to the letting value of the premises, the subsection also allows the landlord to reasonably require, as a condition of such licence or consent, an undertaking on the part of the tenant to reinstate the premises in the condition in which they were before the improvement was executed. The section has no application to covenants which impose an absolute covenant not to effect any improvements. Nor does it apply to mining or agricultural leases.

In determining whether any proposed works are 'improvements' (within s19(2)) or pure alterations, the courts will examine the issue from the tenant's standpoint. It is sufficient that the alterations enhance the tenant's beneficial user of the demised premises even where it diminishes the letting value of the premises (otherwise the provision in s19(2) for paying a reasonable sum for diminution to the reversion would not make sense). In *FW Woolworth and Co Ltd* v *Lambert* (1937), the tenants held a lease of shop premises from the landlords for an unexpired term of 42 years. The lease contained a qualified covenant against the making of any structural alterations to the demised premises without the landlord's consent. The tenants proposed to enlarge the shop by pulling down the wall at the back and connecting it with the other adjoining land of which they held a lease from another landlord. The landlords refused their consent to the alterations except on payment of £7,000 in respect of damage to or diminution in the value of the demised premises. The tenants offered to reinstate the premises in their former condition before the end of the term, and to take out a policy of insurance to secure the performance of this undertaking, but they refused to pay the £7,000. The Court of Appeal held that the proposed alterations were 'improvements' within the meaning of s19(2) and that the tenants had failed to discharge the onus which lay on them of proving that the landlords had unreasonably withheld their consent to the proposed works. The burden of proof, however, will shift if the landlord gives no reason for refusing his consent: *Lambert* v *FW Woolworth & Co Ltd* (1938) (involving the same premises and similar issues). In this second action, the Court of Appeal emphasised that the fact that the improvement involves merger with other premises does not alone take the works out of s19(2) so long as the tenant's beneficial user of the demised premises is thereby enhanced. But it may be otherwise if the alterations of the demised premises are merely *ancillary* to the improvement of other premises.

If the landlord insists that the tenant should pay a sum of money (in respect of diminution in value) on a 'take it or leave it' basis, he is in a dangerous position because, if the tenant proves that the amount is unreasonable, the latter will be free to go ahead with the proposed works without seeking further consent. In other words, the proviso in s19(2), namely, 'such consent not to be unreasonably withheld', operates as a *condition precedent* to the tenant's covenant (ie there is no covenant if the landlord unreasonably withholds consent). In the first action in *Woolworth*, the Court of Appeal held that it had no jurisdiction to determine what would be a reasonable figure for diminution in value. If, therefore, the landlord's objections are confined to diminution in value, it is advisable for him to propose a figure and further propose that, if this figure is not acceptable to the tenant, the matter should be referred to arbitration.

The landlord's objections need not be confined to allegations of likely financial loss (ie he may object on aesthetic or architectural grounds).

In *Haines v Florensa* (1990), the tenant held a long lease of an upper flat of which the freehold reversion was vested in the landlord, who was also the occupier of a garden flat in the building. The lease expressly included the roof in the demise and contained a covenant by the tenant not to carry out alterations without the landlord's consent. The tenant sought the landlord's consent for the conversion of the loft to increase the tenant's usable living space, involving raising the height of the roof and installing a room with a bathroom en suite. The Court of Appeal held that the proposed works were 'improvements' for the purposes of s19(2) and that consent had been unreasonably refused by the landlord. The Court rejected the landlords' argument that the works would cause disruption by way of noise, dirt and disturbance amounting to a nuisance or trespass.

In the context of residential lettings, s610 of the Housing Act 1985 empowers the court to vary the terms of any lease so as to authorise the alteration and/or improvement of the premises. It is also noteworthy that a tenant who wishes to alter, or otherwise build upon, or change the use of the land demised, but is impeded in this regard by a covenant in the lease which prohibits the same may, in certain circumstances, apply to the Lands Tribunal for the discharge or modification of the restriction, pursuant to s84 of the Law of Property Act 1925. The section is commonly used by freehold owners seeking to discharge or modify restrictive covenants which affect their land. However, the same section also empowers certain lessees to make similar application in order that restrictions affecting proposed alterations and improvements to the demised premises may be removed or modified.

5.4.2 *Improvements*

By virtue of Part I of the Landlord and Tenant Act 1927, a business tenant is entitled, in some cases, to compensation for any improvement he makes to the demised property if, before making the improvement, he notifies the landlord of the proposed works. Should the landlord then serve a notice of objection, the tenant may apply to the court to have the proposed improvement certified as a proper improvement. Section 9 provides that Part I of the Act applies notwithstanding any contract to the contrary. It seems, therefore, that Part I will sometimes allow the tenant to circumvent a covenant against alterations, even an absolute covenant: see further, Ch 8, at 8.6.2.

5.5 User

The lease will invariably include a covenant which restricts the possible usage of the demised premises to a particular type of user or a limited class of user purposes (eg 'to keep use and occupy the shop for the trade or business of a [greengrocers] only and not during the term to use exercise or carry on or permit or suffer to be used exercised or carried on in or upon the premises or any part thereof any other trade or business whatsoever').

A user covenant may also be either absolute or qualified. An absolute user restriction prevents the tenant from changing the user of the premises at all (unless the lease is formally varied by deed). A qualified restriction, on the other hand, will permit the tenant to vary the user upon the landlord giving his consent or licence to the change of user. There is no statutory provision which requires the landlord's refusal of consent to be justifiable on the basis of being 'reasonable'. Thus, if consent is not forthcoming, the proposed change of user will not be permissible, unless the tenant can establish that the landlord has acquiesced in the breach of covenant or waived the same.

Alternatively, in the context of a qualified covenant, a landlord may expressly declare that any consent/licence is not to be unreasonably withheld. In the absence of any such express proviso (as already mentioned) there is no statutory implied requirement of reasonableness in relation to a qualified covenant against change of user. However, s19(3) of the Landlord and Tenant Act 1927 prohibits the landlord from demanding from the tenant a 'fine or sum of money in the nature of a fine' (whether by increase of rent or otherwise) for such consent or licence, if the change of user does not involve any structural alteration of the demised premises. The subsection will apply despite any express provision to the contrary contained in the lease. The term 'fine' has been given a wide meaning and includes a stipulation for the giving of a tie in the case of a public house: *Gardner & Co v Cone* (1928). In *Barclays Bank plc v Daejan Investments (Grove Hall) Ltd* (1995), the landlord's consent for a change of user included a proposal that the lease should include a landlord's break clause. This was held to constitute a fine within the meaning of s19(3). If the tenant agrees to pay a fine in consideration of the landlord's granting of consent to a change of user, such an agreement is unenforceable but, somewhat peculiarly, it seems that the tenant cannot recover money paid under the agreement: *Comber v Fleet Electrics Ltd* (1955). The subsection does not preclude the landlord from requiring payment of a reasonable sum in respect of any damage to or diminution in the value of the premises or any neighbouring premises belonging to him and of any legal or other expenses (eg surveyor's fees) incurred in connection with his licence or consent. A civil court is given jurisdiction under s19(3) to determine the reasonableness of any such sum required by the landlord and, once a reasonable sum has been determined, the landlord is bound to grant consent on payment of the sum so determined to be reasonable.

Section 19(3) has no application to mining or agricultural leases: s19(4). It also does not apply to absolute covenants against change of user, or qualified covenants against change of user involving structural alterations of the premises. In such cases, the landlord has absolute freedom to demand a fine.

Leasehold covenants which are restrictive of user may, in certain circumstances, be modified pursuant to s610 of The Housing Act 1985, or modified or discharged by the Lands Tribunal pursuant to s84 of the Law of Property Act 1925 (see 5.4.1).

5.6 Options to renew/purchase

Irrespective of any statutory conferred rights of occupation under Part II of the Landlord and Tenant Act 1954 (see, Ch 8), many commercial leases will contain the seeds of their own reproduction. The right may be in the form of a covenant by the landlord to automatically renew the lease on its expiry or, more commonly, an option conferred on the tenant to renew at his own volition.

The exercise of a tenant's option to renew the lease will typically be made conditional on the tenant's strict observance of his covenants in the lease. In *West Country Cleaners (Falmouth) Ltd* v *Saly* (1966), the tenants of shop premises were given an option to renew the lease for a further term of seven years on giving 12 months' notice before the expiry of the original term provided that there had been due observance and performance by the tenants of all covenants contained in the lease. In breach of the terms of the lease, the tenants had not done any interior painting in the last year of the term. Nevertheless, the premises were kept in a fair state of repair. The Court of Appeal held that an option for renewal of a lease was a privilege which required strict compliance with the terms and conditions upon which it was granted before it could be exercised and, therefore, the tenants were disqualified by reason of their breach of covenant, albeit that the breaches were only trivial, from exercising their option to renew. The material date for determining whether the tenants have complied with the conditions upon which the option to renew the lease is granted is the date of the expiry of the original term and not the date when the tenant gives notice purporting to exercise his option.

To be valid and enforceable, an option to renew the lease must be sufficiently certain. In *King's Motors (Oxford) Ltd* v *Lax* (1969), a lease of a garage filling station and adjoining premises contained an option for the grant of a further term at such rent as might be agreed between the parties. The Court held that, in the absence of an arbitration clause or some supplementary agreement fixing the rent to be paid, the option was void for uncertainty and could not be enforced against the landlords. By contrast, in *Brown* v *Gould* (1972), a vaguely worded option to renew was upheld on the basis that it was capable of having some workable meaning. In this case, the option to renew provided for the grant of a further term of 21 years 'at a rent to be fixed having regard to the market value of the premises at the time of exercising this option…' The option provided no machinery for fixing the rent. The Court, distinguishing the *King's Motors* case, held that it was not precluded from resolving a dispute as to the rent to be made payable if the parties disagreed as to the quantum resulting from the application of a proper formula to the facts of the case.

An option to *purchase* is different from an option to renew in that it is essentially a separate agreement collateral to the lease whereby the tenant is given the means to purchase the landlord's reversionary interest. In the event that the machinery involving the determination of the price breaks down, the court may substitute its own subjective criteria to ascertain what, in all the circumstances, is a 'fair and reasonable price' and, accordingly, compel performance of the option to purchase. In *Sudbrook Trading Estate Ltd* v *Eggleton* (1983), the option to purchase provided that the purchase price was to be 'not less than £12,000 as may be agreed upon by two valuers one to be nominated by the lessor and the other by the lessee and, in default of such agreement, by an umpire appointed by the...valuers'. The tenants exercised the option but the landlords refused to appoint a valuer. The House of Lords held that, on its true construction, the option was for a sale at a fair and reasonable price by the application of objective standards and, once the option had been exercised in accordance with the necessary preconditions, since the price was capable of being ascertained and was thus certain, a complete contract for the sale of the freehold reversion was constituted. Since the price was to be ascertained by machinery which was a subsidiary and non-essential part of the contract, the court would, if the machinery broke down for any reason, substitute its own machinery to ascertain a fair and reasonable price.

Chapter 6

Enforceability of Covenants

6.1 Introduction

This chapter is concerned with the question: who can enforce a
covenant in a lease and against whom? Unfortunately, the question
does not admit of a simple answer because the law now differs
depending on whether the lease was granted before, or on or after
1 January 1996, when the Landlord and Tenant (Covenants) Act
1995 came into force. It will be convenient to examine this topic
from the standpoint of the various parties to the lease.

6.2 Liability of the original tenant

6.2.1 Pre-1996 leases

(a) General law

In relation to leases created prior to 1 January 1996, an original
tenant is, as a matter of contract, legally liable to the landlord on
all the covenants (express or implied) of the lease for the duration
of the term, even where he subsequently assigns his interest.
Invariably, he will covenant expressly on behalf of himself and his
successors in title but, even where this is not the case, he will be
deemed to do so, in respect of those covenants which relate to the
land, by virtue of s79(1) of the Law of Property Act 1925, unless a
contrary intention appears in the lease.

The original tenant's liability will also continue despite an
assignment of the landlord's reversionary interest in the demised
premises. In these circumstances, the assignee of the reversion (ie
the new landlord) is entitled to sue on the covenants in the lease
provided they are real (as opposed to personal) covenants: s141(1)
of the Law of Property Act 1925. The distinction between real and
personal covenants is important in this context because only
covenants which fall within the first category will be binding on an
assignee of the reversion (or lease) by virtue of privity of estate.
Essentially, the covenant will be a real covenant if it affects the

nature, quality, mode of user or value of the demised property: *P & A Swift Investments* v *Combined English Stores Group plc* (1988). Examples of covenants which have been held to be real (ie which 'touch and concern' the land) include (a) to pay rent; (b) to repair the premises; (c) to insure against fire; and (d) for quiet enjoyment. The effect of s141(1) of the 1925 Act is that, once the reversion has been assigned, it is only the assignee of the reversion who can sue on the real covenants, whether the breach took place before or after the assignment: *Re King, (Deceased) Robinson* v *Gray* (1963).

The original tenant will not, however, remain liable on the covenants in the lease during a statutory continuation of a commercial lease under s24 of the Landlord and Tenant Act 1954 see Ch 8, at 8.3, unless the contractual term is expressed to extend to such statutory continuation. The point arose in two related appeals in *City of London Corporation* v *Fell* (1993) and *Herbert Duncan Ltd* v *Cluttons* (1993). In the former, the landlords demised commercial premises to the tenants for a term of ten years from 25 March 1976. In June 1979, the tenants assigned the lease to a company called Grovebell Group plc (the assignee). Although the contractual term expired on 25 March 1986, the assignee remained in possession pursuant to Part II of the Landlord and Tenant Act 1954 (conferring statutory protection on business tenants). In December 1986, the assignee was compulsorily wound up and, in January 1987, it surrendered the tenancy to the landlords. No rent had been paid after the Christmas quarter day 1985. The landlords' claim for the rent arrears against the original tenants was unsuccessful. The Court of Appeal held that, where an original tenant assigned his tenancy before the end of the contractual term, the tenancy which s24(1) of the 1954 Act provides shall not come to an end could only be the tenancy of the assignee. Thus, if the original tenant contracted to pay rent only during the contractual term (as in *Fell*), the landlord could not recover from him any rent in respect of a period of statutory continuation of the term after that date. (The Court of Appeal decision in *Fell* was subsequently upheld by the House of Lords). The position will be different, however, if the contractual term is expressed in the lease to specifically include not only the term thereby granted but also the period of any holding over or any extension thereof whether by statute (ie s24 of the 1954 Act) or at common law. This was the position in the second appeal (*Herbert Duncan*) with the consequence that the original tenant in that case was held liable for the assignee's default. By further contrast to the decision in *Fell*, the original tenant's liability will continue where the contractual term is extended by the exercise of an option contained in the lease: *Baker* v *Merckel* (1960).

In the absence of an express indemnity covenant, there is implied into any assignment of the lease for value a covenant under which the assignee will indemnify the assignor in respect of any liability incurred for any breach of covenant committed during the remainder of the term of the lease: see s77(1)(c) of the Law of Property Act 1925 in the case of unregistered land. In the case of registered land, an indemnity is implied in any transfer: s24(1) of the Land Registration Act 1925. The effect of these provisions is that the original tenant will have a right of indemnity against his immediate assignee and each subsequent assignor will also have a similar right of indemnity against his assignee, thereby creating a chain of indemnity covenants. In addition to this statutory right, the original tenant has an implied right of indemnity at common law against the assignee in breach: *Moule* v *Garrett* (1872).

It has been held that an original tenant has no power to compel an intermediate assignee to sue the current assignee in breach for recovery of arrears of rent: *Re Mirror Group (Holdings) Ltd* (1992). Equally, the original tenant has no power to force the landlord to sue the current assignee in breach before pursuing his remedy against him: *Norwich Union Life Insurance* v *Low Profile Fashions* (1992).

(b) Effect of the 1995 Act

The position prior to the enactment of the Landlord and Tenant (Covenants) Act 1995 was that the liability of the original tenant continued even where the terms of the lease were subsequently varied by the original landlord and an assignee of the lease. In *Selous Street Properties Ltd* v *Oronel Fabrics Ltd* (1984), for example, the landlord brought an action for arrears of rent against, *inter alia*, the original tenants, who contested their liability on the ground that the rent review (under which the unpaid rent arose) had been carried out on a basis different from that to which the original tenants had agreed. In this connection, the landlords had agreed that certain structural alterations made by the assignees in breach of covenant should be allowed to remain as part of the demised premises during the term. The Court held that any increase in the rental value of the premises for rent review purposes did not discharge the liability of the original tenant. The assignee stood in the shoes of the original tenant and was the owner of the whole leasehold estate and, hence, could deal with it so as to alter it or its terms. Similarly, in *GUS Management Ltd* v *Texas Homecare Ltd* (1993) the assignee of the lease had agreed a stepped rent review which was not strictly in accordance with the review provisions in the lease. With the assignee's default, the landlord sued the original tenant, claiming the reviewed rent. The original tenant's argument that its liability was fixed precisely by the terms of the lease and that any deviation from those terms was not binding on it was firmly rejected by the Court. The obvious injustice to tenants stemming from this line of authority has now been remedied by incorporating into the 1995 Act a provision (s18) that no former tenant (or his surety) is liable to pay any sum resulting from a 'relevant variation' to the terms of the lease effected after the enactment of the Act (ie 1 January 1996). Essentially, the liability on former tenants (and their sureties) will only be increased by subsequent variations if either (a) it is contemplated in the lease or (b) it is permitted under the general law (eg the tenant's right to make improvements under s3 of the Landlord and Tenant Act 1927). It is important to note that s18 relates only to changes in the covenants which increase liability of the former tenant (or his surety). The variation must also be one that the landlord had an absolute right to refuse if he wished. An example of a variation that is not covered by s18 is an increase in rent under a rent review clause, because the former tenant (or his surety) would have agreed to such a covenant and the covenant itself has not been altered. By contrast, a variation that is caught by s18 would be the landlord permitting subletting of the demised premises which, prior to the variation, was prohibited under the terms of the lease.

It should be remembered that certain changes (eg extending the term of the lease or addition of further premises) are so fundamental that they operate as a surrender of the old lease and the grant of a new one: *Friends' Provident Life Office* v *British Railways Board* (1996). The consequence of this is that it will give the tenant the benefit of the new privity regime under the 1995 Act!

One of the main provisions of the Landlord and Tenant (Covenants) Act 1995, which applies to all leases (including those entered into before 1 January 1996), requires that, if the landlord wishes to sue the original tenant for fixed charges (ie arrears of rent, service charge or liquidated damages, including interest on any of these sums) he must give notice of his intention to do so within six months of the liability arising: see s17. The landlord must serve notice in respect of each payment, although a notice can cover more than one payment so long as each became due less than six months ago. Failure to do so means that the landlord loses the right to recover from the original tenant to the extent that the sums fell due more than six months prior to any notice served. The landlord does not, of course, have to serve a s17 notice in respect of any liability which is not a fixed charge (eg unliquidated damages in respect of dilapidations). Interestingly, the original tenant is not required to serve a s17 notice on its assignee in order to recover its payments from it: *MW Kellog Ltd* v *F Tobin* (unreported, 8 April 1999).

Another important provision under the 1995 Act, which is common to both old and new leases, relates to the former tenant's entitlement to an 'overriding lease'. The Act entitles the former tenant, if he satisfies an obligation of an assignee following assignment, to call for the grant to him (within 12 months) of an overriding lease from the landlord for a term equal to the unexpired residue of the actual lease (plus a nominal reversion). This has the effect of inserting the former tenant as an intermediate landlord between the landlord and the defaulting assignee. The overriding lease will be on the same terms as the defaulting assignee's lease subject to minor adjustments.

The advantage of the overriding lease to the former tenant is that he will be able to forfeit the assignee's lease and regain possession of the demised premises with a view to marketing them. The rationale behind the overriding lease is, therefore, to give the former tenant the opportunity to recoup his expenditure in discharging his liability to the landlord. On the downside, however, the overriding lease attracts stamp duty (which may be considerable). Also, by taking up such a lease, the former tenant may become liable for significant landlord's covenants (eg to repair, insure, perform maintenance services, etc).

6.2.2 Post-1996 leases

With regard to leases (both commercial and residential) created on or after 1 January 1996, the position is now governed by the Landlord and Tenant (Covenants) Act 1995. (Agreements, court orders and options for tenancies which were entered into before this date are treated as pre-1996 leases). Section 2 of the Act abolishes the distinction between personal and real covenants to be found under the pre-1995 Act law. Covenants under the lease are referred to simply as being either 'landlord covenants' or 'tenant covenants' and these expressions apply to covenants whether express or implied by law. However, where a covenant is expressed to be personal to any party, it is not enforceable under the Act against any other person.

The basic principle under the Act is that, on assignment, the original tenant will be automatically released from his liabilities and only the tenant for the time being will be liable to the landlord. The original tenant, however, remains liable for any breach of covenant occurring before the assignment.

There is one situation in which the tenant will continue to be liable under the covenants of the lease following an assignment. This is where the landlord requires the tenant to enter into an authorised guarantee agreement (AGA), whereby the tenant guarantees performance of the covenants in the lease by his immediate assignee. The AGA must release the tenant from liability under the agreement on a further assignment of the lease. If the tenant is not so released, the agreement is not an AGA and is void under the Act's anti-avoidance provisions. The AGA will be imposed in one of three circumstances:

- Upon the parties negotiating a new lease. The 1995 Act leaves it open to the parties to agree in advance the conditions upon which the landlord will consent to an assignment of the lease. One such condition may be that the tenant enters into an AGA with the landlord prior to assigning the lease;
- The lease contains an absolute prohibition against assignment, but the landlord decides, nevertheless, to permit the proposed assignment but only on condition that the tenant enters into an AGA;
- The lease contains a qualified covenant against assignment (ie the landlord's consent is required to the assignment, which consent cannot be unreasonably withheld) and it is reasonable for the landlord to require the tenant to enter into an AGA as a condition of granting such consent. The circumstances in which it is reasonable for the landlord to impose an AGA (as opposed to some other form of security such as, for example, a rent deposit) remain uncertain in the absence of any judicial guidance (to date) on this question. It is also unclear to what extent the landlord can insist on additional security (eg from the assignee).

The circumstances in which the AGA may be imposed by the landlord are more fully explained in Ch 4, at 4.4. For present purposes, it is important to stress that the tenant's liability under the AGA is entirely different from its previous liability as tenant under the lease before the assignment. The tenant liability is released and replaced by a new liability which is that of a surety only. Thus, his liability will be discharged, for example, upon a subsequent variation of the lease terms (see 6.5, under liability of a surety).

The default notice procedure under s17 of the 1995 Act (see 6.2.1(b)) applies in the context of recovering arrears of rent, service charge and liquidated damages from the former tenant under his liability arising by virtue of an AGA. Equally, the former tenant is entitled to call for an overriding lease if he satisfies his immediate assignee's obligations under the lease by virtue of his AGA commitment. Apart from this, the original tenant may still seek an indemnity for his expenditure from his immediate assignee (under s77 of the Law of Property Act 1925 or s24 of the Land Registration Act 1925), or from the assignee in breach by way of indemnity under the common law rule in *Moule* v *Garret* (1872) (see 6.2.1(a)).

6.3 Liability of the original landlord

6.3.1 Pre-1996 leases

It is frequently overlooked that the privity of contract rule applies to landlords just as it does to tenants. Thus, the original landlord will remain liable to the tenant on his covenants (express or implied) in the lease despite an assignment of the lease: *City & Metropolitan Properties Ltd* v *Greycroft Ltd* (1987). It is also well-established that the original landlord, although he can no longer sue, can still be sued once the reversion has been assigned: *Re King, (Deceased) Robinson* v *Gray* (1963).

6.3.2 Post-1996 leases

Under the 1995 Act, if the landlord wishes to be released from his covenants in the lease when he assigns the reversion, he must serve notice on the tenant giving details of the proposed assignment and indicating that he wishes to be released. The tenant then has four weeks within which to object to the proposed release. If he does not object within that period, then, on completion of the assignment, the landlord will be released. If there is an objection (eg the tenant may fear that the premises will decline under the new landlord), the landlord can apply to the County Court for a declaration that it is reasonable for him to be released.

If the landlord is not released on an assignment of the reversion (because he has not applied for release, or because an objection by the tenant is upheld), the former landlord may, nevertheless, subsequently apply for a release on any *further* assignment of the reversion. It is important that a former landlord (who is not released) imposes on his assignee an obligation to notify him when a further assignment is proposed (and to give details of any such proposed assignment) so as to give the former landlord the opportunity to make an application for release.

If the former landlord is not released (for whatever reason), he will remain liable for his obligations under the lease, but also (it seems) retain the benefit of the tenant's obligations. This may mean that both the current and former landlords will have the right to demand rent, etc. The better view is probably that the former landlord only has the benefit of those tenant obligations which are directly linked to his own duties under the lease. For example, if the current landlord defaults in his obligation to perform services and the former landlord (who was not released) carries them out, then the latter can demand the service charge from the tenant.

6.4 Liability of an assignee

6.4.1 Pre-1996 leases

(a) Assignee of the lease

An assignee of the lease can sue or be sued on the covenants in the lease (which 'touch and concern' the land demised) under the rule in *Spencer*'s case (1583) provided that there is a legal assignment of the lease (or the lease was created for a term of less than three years, in which case a deed is not essential under the rule in *Boyer* v *Warbey* (1953)). He will, however, only be liable for breaches of covenant committed while there is privity of estate between himself and the landlord. He is not, therefore, liable for breaches committed *before* the assignment to him (unless they are continuing breaches, for example, a breach of a covenant to repair), nor for breaches committed *after* a further assignment of the lease by him. Unlike the original tenant, therefore, an assignee of the lease can divest himself of liability to the landlord for future breaches by assigning his lease. It is, however, not uncommon for the landlord to insist that the assignee enters into a direct covenant to pay the rent throughout the term of the lease notwithstanding any further assignment. For example, in *Estates Gazette Ltd* v *Benjamin Restaurants Ltd* (1994), the landlord granted the tenant a licence to assign the premises to an assignee. The licence contained a covenant by the assignee 'to pay the rents reserved by the lease at the time and in manner therein provided for'. The lease reserved a rent 'during the said term hereby granted' and the assignee had also covenanted to observe and perform all the covenants on the lessee's part and the word 'lessee' included the person in whom the term was vested from time to time. It was held that such a covenant, despite containing no express provision to make the assignee's liability extend to breaches committed after further assignment by him (eg by adding the words 'during the residue of the term' or 'during the remainder of the term'), was effective to make the assignee liable for rent becoming due after further assignment by him.

Since the assignee is liable for a continuing (antecedent) breach of covenant (eg a covenant to keep in repair), he has no recourse against his assignor and, moreover, is liable to indemnify him if the landlord elects to sue the assignor for the breach: *Middlegate Properties Ltd* v *Bilbao, Caroline Construction Co Ltd* (1972).

(b) Assignee of the reversion

An assignee of the reversion can be sued upon any real covenants in the lease by virtue of s142(1) of the Law of Property Act 1925. However, s142(1) does not entitle the tenant to claim against the assignee of the reversion in respect of consequential loss occurring prior to the assignment as a result of the assignor's breach of repairing covenant. In *Duncliffe* v *Caerfelin Properties Ltd* (1989), the Court drew a distinction between the continuing obligation to observe the repairing covenant, which was contemplated by s142(1), and a liability for the consequence of past breaches, before the assignment of the reversion, resulting in accrued causes of action for damages. Although under s142(1) the obligation to repair covered the remedying of an accumulation of past disrepair dating from before the assignment, this was to be distinguished from the consequences of past disrepair (eg damage to decorations, carpets and furniture resulting from rainwater penetration) which had become accrued causes of action prior to the assignment.

In *Celsteel Ltd* v *Alton House Holdings Ltd (No 2)* (1987), the Court of Appeal indicated that an assignee of the lease (T1) could sue an assignee of the reversion (L1) where the former became tenant after the assignment of the reversion (by L1).

6.4.2 Post-1996 leases

The provisions of the 1995 Act apply without distinction to original tenants and landlords, and also to those who become tenants or landlords by virtue of an assignment of a tenancy or the reversion to a lease. However, the Act does not apply to an assignment (of the lease or reversion) which arises by operation of law (eg on the death of one of the parties or bankruptcy). It also does not apply to unlawful assignments, for example, in breach of the terms of the lease.

It should be noted that, where a lease has been assigned several times, more than one overriding lease may arise. The following is an illustration: the landlord (L) grants a lease to the tenant (T). It is then assigned to T1, then T2, and finally T3. T3 defaults on the rent. L serves a s17 notice on T who pays up and takes an overriding lease. The chain of title is now L–T–T3. T has the benefit of the covenants given by T1 and T2 to Lso decides not to forfeit the lease. T3 is still in default. T serves a s17 notice on T1 who pays up and takes an overriding lease. The chain of title is now L–T–T1–T3.

6.5 Liability of a surety

6.5.1 Pre-1996 leases

The liability of a surety under the lease is a primary one and not co-extensive with the liability of the tenant. In *Associated Dairies Ltd* v *Pierce* (1983), the surety guaranteed payment of the rent and performance of the covenants in the lease, including the covenant to yield up the demised premises at the end of the term. The landlord obtained judgment against the tenant for possession of the premises, arrears of rent and mesne profits. The trial judge held that the surety was liable for both the landlord's loss of rent and for damages for loss of use of the premises until recovery of possession (ie the period covered by the landlord's claim for mesne profits). The surety argued that he was not liable for damages in respect of the period between service of the writ on the tenant and recovery of possession on the ground that the landlord had elected to sue the tenant in tort (mesne profits being damages for trespass), whereas the surety had only guaranteed contractual obligations. The Court of Appeal, agreeing with the trial judge, concluded that the surety was liable for the loss suffered by the landlord both by non-payment of rent and failure by the tenant to yield up possession of the premises after service of the writ. The latter included mesne profits representing loss of use of the premises until recovery of possession.

The covenant of a surety, guaranteeing the performance of the covenants by the tenant which touch and concern the land (ie which are real covenants), can be enforced by an assignee of the reversion: *Kumar* v *Dunning* (1987) and *P and A Swift Investments* v *Combined English Stores Group plc* (1988).

In the absence of express provision, a surety is not liable for breaches occurring during a statutory continuation of a business lease under Part II of the Landlord and Tenant Act 1954: *A Plesser & Co Ltd* v *Davis* (1983) and *Junction Estates Ltd* v *Cope* (1974).

It is also well settled that any variations in the terms of the lease between the landlord and tenant which could prejudice the surety will discharge the latter from his obligations unless he consents to the variation: *Holme* v *Brunskill* (1878) (substantial alteration in terms of tenancy); *Selous Street Properties Ltd* v *Oronel Fabrics Ltd* (1984) (rent review carried out on a different basis from that to which the original tenant had agreed). Alternatively, the surety covenant may be worded so as to determine the surety's liability once the lease ceases to be vested in the original tenant: *Johnsey Estates Ltd* v *Webb* (1990) (where the surety's obligations were expressed to be limited 'so long as the term hereby granted is vested in the tenant' and, accordingly, could not be enforced in the case of a breach of obligation by the assignee of the term). The operation of a break clause in the lease may also provide the surety with an opportunity to limit the duration of his liability: *William Hill (Southern) Ltd* v *Waller* (1991).

The s17 default notice procedure and the provisions in the Landlord and Tenant (Covenants) Act 1995 relating to the grant of an overriding lease apply to sureties of leases granted both before and after 1 January 1996.

6.5.2 *Post-1996 leases*

The 1995 Act provides that the original tenant's surety will automatically be released from liability to the same extent as the tenant, where the latter is himself released upon an assignment of the lease. The surety's liabilities will not be affected, however, where the tenant negotiates a voluntary release from an obligation by the landlord. In this circumstance, whether or not the surety is released will depend on the true construction of the surety covenant in the normal way.

As mentioned above, the s17 notice procedure applies not only to former tenants but also their sureties so that the landlord is obliged to serve notice on them within six months of when the relevant fixed charge(s) fell due. If a surety discharges the liability, he may claim an overriding lease (see 6.5.1).

6.6 Disclaimer of leases

6.6.1 Pre-1996 leases

The effect of a disclaimer of the lease by the liquidator of an insolvent company is laid down by s178(4) of the Insolvency Act 1986, which provides that a disclaimer operates so as to determine (as from the date of disclaimer) the rights, interests and liabilities of the company in the property disclaimed, but does *not* affect the rights or liabilities of any other person. Section 178(6) also provides that any person sustaining loss or damage in consequence of the operation of a disclaimer is deemed to be a creditor of the company to the extent of such loss or damage and, accordingly, may prove for the loss or damage in the company's winding up. There are provisions in identical terms contained in s315 of the 1986 Act in relation to a disclaimer by the trustee in bankruptcy of an individual bankrupt. It will be convenient to consider the effect of these provisions in a case where (a) the lease is vested in the original tenant immediately before the disclaimer and (b) where it is vested in an assignee of the original tenant.

(a) Lease vested in original tenant

A disclaimer by the liquidator (or trustee in bankruptcy) of the original tenant will determine the lease and the tenant's obligations thereunder from the date of disclaimer. The position, until recently, was that the liability of any surety for the lease *in futuro* was also discharged: *Stacey* v *Hill* (1901). The decision in *Stacey* has now been overruled by the House of Lords with the consequence that the disclaimer will *not* affect the obligations to the landlord of a surety of the original (insolvent) tenant. Under s178(4) of the 1986 Act, the interest of the insolvent tenant in the disclaimed property is determined by the disclaimer and the lease extinguished so far as he is concerned, but the lease is deemed to continue in respect of the rights and obligations of other persons: *Hindcastle Ltd* v *Barbara Attenborough Associates Ltd* (1996).

(b) Lease vested in assignee

If the liquidation (or bankruptcy) is that of the assignee of the lease, the disclaimer has the effect of determining the assignee's rights, interests and liabilities in the lease: s178(4) of the 1986 Act (see 6.6.1(a)). In other words, the disclaimer extinguishes the liability of the assignee to pay the rent and replaces it by the different and distinct statutory liability (under s178(6), see 6.6.1) to compensate any party who has sustained loss or damage in consequence of the disclaimer. The effect of the disclaimer is, therefore, merely to terminate the rights, interests and liabilities of the assignee and not the lease itself. The term continues to subsist, although apparently having no owner, until a vesting order is made. Such a lease has been described as being 'something like a dormant volcano which may break out into active operation at any time': *Re Thompson and Cottrell's Contract* (1943).

The disclaimer of the assignee's lease will have no effect, however, on the continuing liability of the original tenant or his surety: *Hill v East and West India Dock Co* (1884). The basis of the decision in *Hill* is that the liability of the original tenant is primary and direct and not dependent on the continued liability of the assignee in possession. Thus, in *Warnford Investments Ltd v Duckworth* (1979), the landlords granted the tenants a lease of business premises for a term of 20 years. Later, with the consent of the landlords, the tenants assigned the lease to a company which went into liquidation and the liquidator disclaimed the lease. The Court held that, when the liquidator of a company disclaimed the lease which had been assigned to the company, the original tenant remained liable to the landlord for the rent throughout the term because the disclaimer, though releasing the company from liability, did not release the original tenant whose rights and liabilities remained unaffected. The result would have been the same if the assignment had been made to an individual and the lease had been disclaimed by his trustee in bankruptcy. Similarly, in *WH Smith Ltd v Wyndham Investments Ltd* (1994), the original tenant assigned the lease to a company which subsequently became insolvent and the liquidator disclaimed the lease. The Court held that the original tenant continued to be liable for the rent after the assignee company had gone into liquidation and the liquidator had disclaimed the lease.

The effect of the disclaimer of the assignee's lease on the *assignee's surety* will depend largely on the wording of the surety covenant. If the surety's obligations are stated to be independent of the covenants of the assignee, then it is clear that they will survive the disclaimer and the surety will continue to be liable. If, however, the liability of the surety is stated to arise only on a *default* of the assignee, then the situation is different. In *Murphy* v *Sawyer-Hoare* (1993), the liability of the assignee's surety arose only in the event of default on the part of the assignee to perform the contractual obligations in the lease. After the date of disclaimer (by operation of s178(4) of the 1986 Act) there could be no such default by the assignee and, consequently, the surety's liability could not survive the disclaimer. (It is interesting to observe that the decision in *Harding* v *Preece* (1882), in which an assignee's surety was held liable for rent accrued due after the disclaimer to the original tenant to whom he had given a guarantee, was not cited). It is evident from *Murphy* that the precise extent of the surety's liabilities in this context will depend upon the true construction of the covenant he has given. It should be stressed, however, that a disclaimer will not affect the liability of a surety in respect of rent accrued due *prior* to the date of disclaimer.

6.6.2 *Post-1996 leases*

In respect of leases granted on or after 1 January 1996, the basic rule, as mentioned earlier, is that the original tenant and his surety will automatically be released from their respective liabilities on assignment of the lease. If the original tenant (or surety) continues to remain liable by virtue of the imposition of an AGA, and the assignee's lease is disclaimed, the original tenant (or surety) may be entitled to an overriding lease under s19 of the Landlord and Tenant (Covenants) Act 1995 (see 6.2.1(b)).

6.7 Liability of and to a stranger to the lease

Under the rule in *Tulk* v *Moxhay* (1848), restrictive covenants are enforceable by injunction even where there is no privity of contract or estate between the parties. The situation may arise, for example, where there is a covenant in the headlease against a particular trade or business and the subtenant in occupation is carrying on that trade or business, his own sublease containing no such restriction. In order for the covenant to be enforceable, however, it must be negative in substance, it must be intended to run with the land demised (this is now presumed under s78 of the Law of Property

Act 1925 unless a contrary intention appears), and the subtenant must have had notice of it (ie it will not bind a *bona fide* purchaser of the legal estate for value without notice of the restriction). Since a subtenant is entitled to call for the title of the headlease, he will be fixed with *constructive* notice of the restriction. But a sub-underlesseee or assignee of sublease will not be bound without *actual* notice, except where he has a contractual right to call for the headlease: s44 of the Law of Property Act 1925.

It should also be noted that adjacent tenants under a letting scheme are entitled to enforce *inter se* restrictive covenants imposed on them in their leases under the scheme, even though they are strangers, under the rule in *Elliston* v *Reacher* (1908).

Positive covenants are, generally speaking, unenforceable in the absence of privity of contract or estate between the parties. An exception to this rule is where the tenant elects to take some reciprocal benefit arising under the covenant: see *Halsall* v *Brizell* (1957).

The power of the Lands Tribunal to modify or discharge restrictive covenants under s84 of the Law of Property Act 1925 does not apply to leasehold covenants except where the lease (other than a mining lease) was granted for a term exceeding 40 years and 25 years or more have expired: s52 of the Landlord and Tenant Act 1954.

Where the covenant is only enforceable in equity, an injunction may be refused on equitable considerations where, for example, (a) by reason of changes in the neighbourhood, the covenant has become valueless to the landlord, or (b) the landlord, by his acts or omissions has, in effect, represented that the covenants are no longer enforceable (ie implied release): see *Chatsworth Estates Ltd* v *Fewell* (1931) and *Sobey* v *Sainsbury* (1913).

6.8 The Contracts (Rights of Third Parties) Bill

The Bill (which will become law in late 1999) provides that a third party may enforce directly a contractual term where the contract expressly provides that right or where the contractual term confers a benefit on him. These new provisions will have an important effect on the enforcement of leasehold covenants.

The Bill allows for the inclusion of subtenants, as a named class of future persons, as the beneficiaries of covenants in a headlease granted after the Bill becomes law. In other words, the subtenant will be able to enforce the head landlord's covenants directly against the superior landlord. Equally, the superior landlord will be able to enforce the covenants of the headlease against the subtenant.

Chapter 7

Termination of Leases

7.1 Introduction

There are a number of different ways in which a commercial lease or tenancy agreement may validly be brought to an end. These are detailed below.

7.2 Forfeiture

The forfeiture of the lease is, of course, the primary remedy of a landlord faced with a tenant who has defaulted in the payment of his rent or other obligations in the lease. At the same time, the lease will invariably be a valuable asset which the tenant will seek to preserve in most cases by seeking relief against forfeiture. There is a vast body of case law on the subject as well as several important statutory provisions.

In 1985, the Law Commission, as part of its programme for the codification of the law of landlord and tenant, published a report entitled '*Forfeiture of Tenancies*' (Law Com No 142), which examined various defects in the current law and recommended the replacement of the present structure with an entirely new system. In 1994, the Commission published a further report (*Landlord and Tenant Law: Termination of Tenancies Bill*, Law Com No 221, 1994) which contains a draft bill implementing the Commission's proposals. In 1998, the Commission published a consultative document recommending various amendments to its original proposal regarding the landlord's current right to forfeit by physical re-entry onto the demised premises. It may still be some time, however, before the Bill actually becomes law.

The right of the landlord to forfeit a business tenancy is expressly preserved by s24(2) of the Landlord and Tenant Act 1954. Where, however, there is a judgment for forfeiture and a subsisting application for relief from forfeiture (see 7.2.5), the business tenancy does not 'come to an end by forfeiture' for the purposes of s24(2) until the final outcome of the proceedings: *Meadows* v *Clerical, Medical and General Life Assurance Society* (1981).

7.2.1 *When does the right of forfeiture arise?*

The landlord has a right to forfeit in the following circumstances:

- *Under a proviso for re-entry*. Invariably, the lease will contain a forfeiture clause entitling the landlord to re-enter the demised property and terminate the lease upon the tenant's failure to pay rent, his insolvency, or other breaches of covenant (eg repair, user, alterations, insurance, etc);
- *Where the tenant denies his landlord's title*. This may arise in three distinct circumstances. First, where the tenant, in the course of his pleadings, expressly denies the landlord's title and is thereby prevented from re-asserting his lease or tenancy. Secondly, where the tenant deliberately attempts to set up an adverse (or hostile) title either in himself or in a third party in the face of the landlord's title. Thirdly, where there is a disclaimer of the lease (by words or acts) by a yearly or other periodic tenant which will operate as a waiver by the tenant of the usual notice to quit. The effect of such a disclaimer is that the landlord may terminate the tenancy forthwith without serving the appropriate notice to quit;
- *Upon the happening of an event specified in an express condition in the lease*. Where the particular stipulation in the lease falls to be construed as a condition (as opposed to a covenant), the landlord will be entitled to forfeit the lease upon the happening of the event specified in the condition without recourse to a proviso for re-entry contained in the lease. Today, the most common condition included amongst the terms of a lease, is the condition which entitles the landlord to forfeit the lease if the tenant becomes bankrupt or goes into liquidation or permits other associated events (eg composition with creditors) to occur during the currency of the term. Such a condition, however, is invariably to be found in the proviso for re-entry in any event in order to permit forfeiture for breach of covenant. As such, it is not a typical condition in the classical sense because conditions of the latter kind are imposed independently of any forfeiture clause in the lease and give rise to an automatic right of forfeiture;
- *Under s35(2) of the Sexual Offences Act 1956*. Where the tenant is convicted of knowingly permitting the whole or part of the demised premises to be used as a brothel, the landlord has a statutory right to determine the lease if the tenant fails to assign it within three months of being required to do so by the landlord.

7.2.2 *Who may assert a right of forfeiture?*

The effect of s4 of the Landlord and Tenant (Covenants) Act 1995 (formerly s141 of the Law of Property Act 1925), is that an assignee of the reversion can sue and re-enter the demised premises in respect of a breach committed before (or after) the assignment. Once the right of the landlord to enforce breaches of covenant has effectively passed to the assignee of the reversion, the former landlord will no longer, after the date of the assignment, have any right to enforce a right of re-entry against the tenant.

7.2.3 *Exercise of the right of forfeiture*

In order to bring about an effective forfeiture of the lease, the landlord must take some positive and unequivocal step to signify to the tenant his intention of treating the lease as at an end as a consequence of the tenant's default. This may be done either by physically re-entering on to the demised premises or by suing for possession. If the landlord adopts the former method, he must be careful not to infringe the provisions of s6 of the Criminal Law Act 1977, which prohibit the landlord from using or threatening violence for the purposes of securing entry on to the premises where there is someone present on those premises at the time who is opposed to the entry. (Moreover, actual re-entry is not available to a landlord where the premises are let as a dwelling and while any person is lawfully residing therein: s2 of the Protection from Eviction Act 1977). In view of these difficulties, the more usual course in practice is for the landlord to initiate proceedings for possession where the service of the proceedings will operate in law as a notional re-entry.

The issue of the proceedings against the tenant claiming possession of the demised premises will operate as a final and conclusive election by the landlord to forfeit the lease. Consequently, he will be precluded from enforcing any subsequent breach of covenant against the tenant unless the conduct complained of is also tortious (ie amounts to a nuisance or trespass, or is negligent). The landlord cannot rely upon any subsequent breach because, having elected to forfeit the lease, he is effectively estopped (or prevented) from treating the lease (and the covenants in the lease) as still on foot. The tenant, on the other hand, is in a different position. From his standpoint, the landlord's covenants remain 'potentially good' pending the final determination of the landlord's forfeiture action so that, notwithstanding the forfeiture, the tenant may continue to enforce the landlord's covenants pending the outcome of his application for relief from forfeiture. The conceptual nature of the lease during this 'twilight period' (ie between its forfeiture and the determination of the tenant's application for relief from forfeiture) has been the subject of judicial comment. For example, in *Liverpool Properties Ltd* v *Oldbridge Investments Ltd* (1985), Parker LJ observed that 'there is a period of limbo during which it cannot be predicted for a certainty whether the lease will ever truly come to an end, for if there is a counterclaim for relief…and that counterclaim for relief succeeds and any conditions are complied with, the original lease continues'.

In cases involving forfeiture for non-payment of rent, the common law requires a formal demand for the rent as a pre-requisite to forfeiture. This requirement is rendered unnecessary, however, where at least six months' rent is in arrears before the date of the service of proceedings and no sufficient distress is to be found on the demised premises countervailing the arrears then due: s210 of the Common Law Procedure Act 1852 and s139 of the County Courts Act 1984. The requirement of a formal demand can be (and in practice always is) dispenesed with in any event by reserving a right of re-entry for non-payment of rent 'whether formally demanded or not'.

In cases involving forfeiture for other breaches of covenant (ie not involving non-payment of rent), the landlord cannot forfeit unless he has first served notice (under s146(1) of the Law of Property Act 1925) on the tenant (a) specifying the particular breach complained of; (b) if the breach is capable of remedy, requiring the tenant to remedy the breach; and (c) in any case, requiring the tenant to make compensation for the breach. The s146 notice must provide sufficient detail of the breach as would enable the tenant to understand within reasonable certainty what it is he is required to do so that he has an opportunity of remedying the breach before the landlord proceeds to forfeit: *Fox* v *Jolly* (1916) applied in *Adagio Properties Ltd* v *Ansari* (1998), involving a breach of a covenant against alterations.

Where the breach of covenant is capable of remedy, the notice itself need not specify the time within which the breach is to be remedied since s146(1) merely precludes the landlord from enforcing his right of forfeiture until expiry of a reasonable period of time from the date of the service of his notice. The reason for giving the tenant 'reasonable' notice under s146(1) is not, however, limited to giving him the opportunity to remedy the breach. It is also to enable him to consider his legal position and whether or not to apply for relief against forfeiture. A breach of a positive covenant (eg failure to repair) will ordinarily be remediable provided such remedy is carried out within a reasonable period of time, which in turn will depend on the particular circumstances of the case: *Expert Clothing Service & Sales Ltd* v *Hillgate House Ltd* (1986).

Some breaches, however, are considered, as a matter of law, as being *incapable* of remedy. Thus, a breach of a negative covenant which leaves a 'stigma' on the demised premises is generally incapable of remedy (eg use of premises for an illegal or immoral purpose). The rationale here is that such breaches can only be effectively remedied by the tenant vacating the premises. A breach of covenant not to assign, sublet, or part with possession of the demised property is also a breach not capable of remedy within the meaning of s146(1): *Scala House & District Property Co Ltd* v *Forbes* (1974). Where the breach is characterised as incapable of remedy, the s146 notice need not require the tenant to remedy it and the landlord may proceed with his action (or physical re-entry) with little delay. In such circumstances, it has been held that 14 days is a sufficient time to elapse between the service of the notice and commencement of proceedings for forfeiture: see the *Scala* case, above.

The decision in *Hillgate* (above) left open the argument that if a breach of a negative covenant does not involve any lingering stigma or taint on the premises (eg a breach of covenant not to make alterations to the demised premises) then the breach may be capable of remedy. The point was recently addressed in *Savva* v *Hussein* (1997), where the Court of Appeal held that, in the case of covenants not to make alterations, or not to display signs, without consent, if there is a breach the mischief can be removed by removing the signs or restoring the property to the state it was in before the alterations.

Where the breach involves a breach of a covenant to repair, the s146 notice must also comply with the Leasehold Property (Repairs) Act 1938, where the Act applies: see Ch 3, at p39.

7.2.4 *Waiver of forfeiture*

Instead of electing to forfeit, the landlord may decide to treat the lease as continuing and waive the forfeiture. If, with knowledge of the breach, a landlord acknowledges to his tenant the continued existence of the lease, he will be taken to have elected not to forfeit.

The rules regarding waiver may operate harshly against the landlord. For example, knowledge of the breach by the landlord's agent will be sufficient even where the act of acknowledgment of the lease is that of another agent who is unaware of the breach. In *Central Estates (Belgravia) Ltd* v *Woolgar (No 2)* (1972), the tenant was convicted of unlawfully keeping a brothel on the demised premises. The landlords' agents, knowing of the tenant's conviction, made internal office arrangements that no further rent should be demanded or accepted from the tenant. By a clerical error, a demand for a quarter's rent was sent out which the tenant paid and for which he was given a receipt. The Court of Appeal held that the landlords' demand for and acceptance of rent through their agents with knowledge of the breach effected a waiver of forfeiture.

Because the consequence of a particular act relied on as a waiver is a matter of law and not the parties' intention, the landlord cannot avoid a waiver by accepting or demanding rent 'under protest' or 'without prejudice' to his right of re-entry: *Windmill Investments (London) Ltd* v *Milano Restaurants Ltd* (1962) and *Segal Securities Ltd* v *Thoseby* (1963). There will also be a waiver where the landlord waives the forfeiture by conduct even though the lease specifically requires a waiver to be expressed in writing: *R* v *Paulson* (1921).

The effect of a waiver will depend on the nature of the breach giving rise to the landlord's election to forfeit. In this connection, the tenant's breach will be classified either as a 'continuing' breach or, alternatively, as a 'once and for all breach'. If the breach is of the former type, there is a continually recurring cause of forfeiture and the waiver will operate only in relation to past breaches (ie breaches committed in the period prior to the landlord's act which constitutes the waiver). The landlord's right of forfeiture will only be barred by evidence of acts of waiver which are so continuous or prolonged as to amount to a new agreement for letting or a licence or release of the tenant's covenant: *Wolfe* v *Hogan* (1949). Examples of breaches which are of a continuing nature include: (a) breach of a user covenant; (b) breach of a covenant to repair; and (c) breach of a covenant to insure.

Where the breach is classified not as a continuing one, but as a once and for all breach, the right to forfeit for that breach will be lost upon waiver. Generally speaking, if the relevant obligation is to perform an act by a given date or within a reasonable period of time, it will fall to be classified as an obligation that can only be broken once: *Farimani* v *Gates* (1984). Examples of covenants which can only be broken once include: (a) a covenant to build before a stated date; (b) a covenant against assigning, subletting, parting with possession; and (c) a covenant not to make alterations.

The various acts on the part of the landlord which have been held to constitute a waiver of forfeiture include:

- Demand for rent due *after* the breach;
- Acceptance of rent due *after* the breach. It appears that the payment of rent into the landlord's bank account, if usual, will operate as a waiver even though the landlord has instructed the bank not to receive it. The decision in *Pierson* v *Harvey* (1885) highlights the importance of the landlord taking appropriate steps to repay the moneys as soon as they are paid into his account and of giving appropriate notice to the tenant (as opposed to merely his bank) that the rent would not be received. In *John Lewis Properties plc* v *Viscount Chelsea* (1993), the bank's action in crediting the tenant's cheques to the landlord's account was held not to amount in law to a waiver because (a) the landlord had informed the tenant that it would not accept rent because of the breaches and (b) once informed of the payments, had consistently rejected them;
- Distraining for rent whenever due;
- Electing to pursue a claim consistent with the continuation of the lease;
- Service of a notice to quit;
- Offer to purchase the tenant's interest;
- Acceptance of surrender of the headlease.

The various acts on the part of the landlord which have been held *not* to amount to a waiver include:

- Receipt of rent due *prior* to the breach;
- Acceptance of rent or levying distress *after* service of the proceedings;
- Service of a notice under s146(1);
- Entering into without prejudice negotiations;
- Mere inactivity;
- Assignment of the reversion expressed to be subject to the lease.

7.2.5 Relief from forfeiture

Even if a ground of forfeiture exists (and has not been waived), it does not necessarily follow that the landlord will be successful in his claim to recover possession of the premises. Both equity and statute law have intervened so as to provide the tenant with the right to apply for relief from forfeiture of the lease. The forms of relief differ depending on whether the landlord claims forfeiture for non-payment of rent or for breach of other covenants in the lease.

(a) Relief against forfeiture for non-payment of rent

From earliest times, equity recognised that it had jurisdiction to relieve against forfeiture where the object of the forfeiture clause was to secure payment of a definite sum of money. This equitable jurisdiction remains intact to this day subject only to various statutory provisions which have merely modified equity's power to grant relief in certain procedural aspects. These provisions differ as between High Court and County Court.

Under s212 of the Common Law Procedure Act 1852, applicable to High Court actions, the tenant may avoid a forfeiture by paying all the arrears and costs to the landlord (or into court) before the trial. The effect of so doing will be to stay the landlord's action. In order, however, for the section to apply, there must be at least six months' rent in arrears. No such limitation is to be found in s138(2) of the County Courts Act 1984, which governs actions in the County Court. Under s138(2), however, the payment of all arrears and costs must be made not less than five clear days before the hearing.

Under s210 of the 1852 Act, applicable to High Court cases, the tenant is also entitled to relief in equity *at* or *after* the trial of the landlord's action, if he pays all the arrears of rent and landlord's costs of the action within six months of the execution of the order for possession. Where, however, there is less than six months' rent in arrears, the six months' limitation period does not apply so as to confine the tenant to a period of six months after execution of the order for possession in which to bring his application for relief. In such circumstances, the court's inherent equitable jurisdiction will apply without strict statutory time-limit, although the six month time-limit prescribed under s210 of the 1852 Act is usually taken as a guide in the exercise of the court's discretion whether to grant or refuse relief. In practice, the court will invariably grant relief to the tenant upon payment of the rent due and the landlord's costs of the action.

Where the landlord proceeds to forfeit the lease for non-payment of rent by *physically re-entering* on to the premises without recourse to legal proceedings, the above statutory provisions will have no application and the tenant will be entitled to rely upon equitable relief without any fixed (statutory) time-limit. In such circumstances, however, relief may be refused on equitable grounds where, for example, the tenant has unduly delayed in bringing his application for relief.

In the County Court, relief is based upon the making of a suspended order for possession. Under s139(3) of the County Courts Act 1984, where the tenant seeks relief at the trial of the landlord's action, the court is obliged to order possession at the expiration of such period, not being less than four weeks from the date of the order, as the court thinks fit, unless within that period the tenant pays into court all the rent in arrears and the costs of the action. The court has power, under s138(4), to extend the period for payment at any time before possession of the premises is recovered by the landlord. If the tenant pays the rent due and costs within the time fixed under the order (or any extension thereof), he will continue to hold under the lease but, if he fails to pay within the time-limit, the order for possession will be enforced and the tenant will be barred from all relief (including relief in the High Court). Under s138(9A) of the 1984 Act, however, the tenant has the right to apply for relief at any time within six months from the date on which the landlord recovers possession of the premises.

Where the landlord forfeits the lease by *physically re-entering* on to the premises, s139(2) of the 1984 Act expressly confers on the County Court the same equitable power to relieve against forfeiture for non-payment of rent as the High Court could have granted, provided that the application for relief is made within six months from the date of the landlord's re-entry.

In addition to relief being available to the tenant, relief may be granted to subtenants and mortgagees who derive title from him. Thus, in the High Court, a subtenant or mortgagee may obtain relief under ss210 and 212 of the 1852 Act. The form of relief is to revive the old lease in favour of the subtenant. In addition, he may apply for relief under s146(4) of the Law of Property Act 1925 at any time before the landlord has actually obtained possession of the premises pursuant to an order of the court. Under s146(4), the court may make an order vesting a new lease in favour of the subtenant or mortgagee in which the covenants and conditions as to rent and otherwise will be entirely at the discretion of the court unfettered by any limitation except that contained in the latter part of the subsection, namely, that a subtenant shall not be entitled to require a lease for a term longer than he had under his original sublease. In the County Court, the right of a subtenant or mortgagee to apply for relief from forfeiture for non-payment of rent under s146(4) is expressly preserved by s138(10) of the 1984 Act. Moreover, where the landlord is proceeding by physical re-entry without action, an application under s139(2) of the 1984 Act may be made by a person with an interest derived from the tenant and the court may make an order which (subject to such terms and conditions as it thinks fit) vests the land in such person for the remainder of the term of the lease or for any less term: s139(3).

(b) Relief against forfeiture otherwise than for non-payment of rent

The general statutory provisions relevant to relief against forfeiture from breaches of covenant (other than non-payment of rent) are contained in s146(2) of the Law of Property Act 1925. The court may grant or refuse relief, on terms, as it thinks fit and, in the case of a breach of repairing covenant, the court will usually require the tenant to remedy the disrepair and make compensation to the landlord for any damage to the reversion before it grants such relief: see further, Ch 3, at p40.

The tenant may apply for relief under s146(2) where the landlord is proceeding to forfeit by court action or by physical re-entry: *Billson v Residential Apartments Ltd* (1992). Section 146(2) provides that the court may grant or refuse relief, having regard to the proceedings and conduct of the parties and to all other circumstances, as it thinks fit. Moreover, in case of relief, the court may grant it on 'such terms, if any, as to costs, expenses, damages, compensation, penalty, or otherwise, including the grant of an injunction to restrain any like breach in the future' as, in the circumstances of each case, it thinks fit. The court's discretion to grant or refuse relief is very wide and will usually depend on any one or more of the following factors:

- Whether the tenant is able and willing to remedy and/or recompense the landlord for the breach;
- Whether the breach was wilful (ie deliberate as opposed to an innocent breach);
- Whether the breach involves an immoral/illegal user;
- The gravity of the breach;
- The extent of the diminution in the value of the landlord's reversionary interest as compared with the value of the leasehold interest threatened with forfeiture;
- The conduct of the landlord;

- The personal qualifications of the tenant;
- The financial position of the tenant.

If relief is granted by the court, the tenant will retain his lease as if it had never been forfeited. The court may, in the exercise of its discretion in granting relief against forfeiture under s146(2), order the payment by the tenant of the landlord's costs and expenses of employing a solicitor and surveyor to prepare a s146 notice (including a schedule of dilapidations). Under s146(3), such reasonable costs and expenses are also recoverable where the court grants relief under s146(2) or where the landlord waives the breach at the tenant's request. If, however, the tenant complies with the landlord's s146 notice by remedying the breach and so avoids the forfeiture, s146(3) will have no application. In order to avoid this difficulty, it is common practice to insert in the lease an express covenant which obliges the tenant to pay all expenses (including solicitors' costs and surveyors' fees) incurred by the landlord incidental to the preparation and service of a s146 notice.

Relief is also available, under s146(4) of the 1925 Act, to holders of derivative interests including subtenants and mortgagees. However, relief is not available after the landlord has recovered possession. If relief is granted, it takes the form of a new lease granted to the applicant.

(c) Relief against forfeiture on tenant's bankruptcy

Special provisions apply in cases involving relief against forfeiture on the tenant's bankruptcy or the taking in of his lease in execution. Section 146(10) provides that the protection of s146 applies for one year from the date of the bankruptcy or taking in execution. If the tenant's interest is not sold within that year, the protection ceases and the section will no longer apply. If, however, the tenant's interest is sold during the year, the protection will continue indefinitely for the benefit of the new tenant. The effect of the provision is to encourage a sale within a year and to enable a sale within that period to be made at a price which is not depressed by the purchaser's fear of having to face an action for possession by the landlord without statutory protection.

7.3 Surrender of the lease

Surrender is the process by which a tenant gives up his leasehold

estate to his immediate landlord. The lease is essentially destroyed by mutual agreement. A surrender may arise expressly or by operation of law.

7.3.1 Express surrender

An express surrender of a term of more than three years must be made by deed: s52(1) of the Law of Property Act 1925. Otherwise, the surrender must be in writing: s53(1)(a) of the 1925 Act. No particular language indicating a surrender is prescribed but words such as 'surrender and yield up' are considered appropriate. Surrenders must operate immediately and cannot be future or conditional.

7.3.2 Surrender by operation of law

An implied surrender by operation of law is expressly exempted from the requirements of a deed or writing: s52(2)(c) and s53(1)(a) of the 1925 Act. Such a surrender may arise from any unequivocal conduct of the parties which is inconsistent with the continuation of the lease.

A common example of such a surrender is where the tenant abandons the premises and the landlord accepts his implied offer of a surrender by changing the locks and re-letting the premises to a third party. The abandonment must, however, be of a permanent and not temporary nature. A mere temporary abandonment is too equivocal unless the tenant is absent for a long time with large rent arrears owing: *Preston Borough Council* v *Fairclough* (1982). Another example of a surrender by operation of law will arise where the tenant agrees with the landlord to replace his existing lease with a new lease on different terms or with substantially different premises: *Bush Transport Ltd* v *Nelson* (1987). A mere variation in the rent, however, will not give rise to a surrender by implication: *Jenkin R Lewis & Son Ltd* v *Kerman* (1971).

In surrendering his lease, a tenant cannot prejudice the rights of other parties affected by it. For example, s139 of the Law of Property Act 1925 provides that, in the event of a surrender of the headlease by a mesne tenant, the superior landlord automatically becomes the landlord in relation to the subtenant so as to preserve the validity of the sublease.

Following a surrender, a tenant may remain liable for past breaches of covenant occurring during the term of his lease: *Richmond* v *Savill* (1926). It is possible, however, for the parties to agree that all past (as well as future) liability of the tenant should cease upon surrender.

A business tenancy can be brought to an end by surrender provided that the deed of surrender is not executed before, or is not executed in pursuance of an agreement to surrender made before, the tenant has been in occupation for one month: s24(2) of the Landlord and Tenant Act 1954: see further, Ch 8, at p117.

7.4 Expiry of time

A lease is determined automatically when the term expires. Under common law principles, a tenant will usually become a trespasser after such expiry. Alternatively, the tenant may hold over as a tenant at will (see Ch 1, at 1.4) or, if the rent is paid and accepted for any given period or periods, as a periodic tenant. Moreover, on the expiry of the tenancy, the tenant will invariably be entitled to continue in occupation by virtue of a statutory privilege or continuation of the contractual term. In relation to business tenancies, the term is automatically continued under s24 of the Landlord and Tenant Act 1954 provided that the tenant is in occupation of the holding for the purposes of his business on the expiry date of the lease: see further, Ch 8, at 8.3.

7.5 Notice to quit

The common law has long accepted that a periodic tenancy is determinable by a notice to quit of appropriate length, served by either landlord or tenant on the other party. The period of notice required (in the absence of any statutory or express provision) is that which corresponds in time to the length of the particular periodic tenancy in question. Thus, weekly periodic tenancies require a notice to quit of one week, monthly tenancies a notice to quit of one month's duration, and so on. However, the termination of yearly periodic tenancies provides a significant exception to this rule as tenancies from year to year require six months' (182 days or two quarter's) notice to quit.

It is essential to the validity of a notice to quit that it should be certain (ie that there should be plain and unambiguous words providing for the determination of the tenancy at a certain time). The general test to be applied in determining the validity of a notice to quit is whether a reasonable tenant would have understood the notice: *Carradine Properties Ltd* v *Aslam* (1976).

A business tenant may terminate his periodic tenancy by giving notice to quit to his landlord. However, a notice to quit given before the tenant has been in occupation as tenant for one month is invalid: see Ch 8, at p116.

7.6 Abandonment of premises

A common example of surrender by operation of law arises when the tenant abandons the premises and the landlord accepts his implied offer of a surrender by re-taking possession, changing the locks and re-letting to a new tenant. The difficulty, however, in most cases is that the tenant's abandonment may be equivocal, especially if the tenant has not been absent for a long time and has left some (or all) of his chattels on the premises. In these circumstances, re-taking possession by the landlord may be unjustified and constitute a trespass onto the demised premises.

Moreover, abandonment by the tenant will not of itself entitle the landlord to forfeit the lease unless it amounts to a breach of covenant. Invariably, in such circumstances, the tenant will have absconded without paying rent so that the landlord will have a ground of forfeiture based on non-payment of rent which will entitle him (assuming that formal demand has been dispensed with or statutorily excepted) to physically re-enter the premises without the necessity of a formal notice under s146(1) of the Law of Property Act 1925 (see above). Moreover, assuming the premises have been abandoned, there will be no statutory restrictions (see s6 of the Criminal Law Act 1997, at 7.2.3) on his right to exercise actual re-entry.

In the case of any breach (other than non-payment of rent), the landlord will be obliged to serve a s146 notice on the tenant although, except where the breach is of a repairing covenant (see s18(2) of the Landlord and Tenant Act 1927), there will be no necessity to show that the notice actually reached the tenant: s196 of the Law of Property Act 1925 and s1 of the Recorded Delivery Service Act 1962.

Apart from relying on the law of forfeiture, the landlord may have resort to s16 of the Distress for Rent Act 1737, which provides a means by which a landlord may, in certain circumstances, recover possession of premises left unoccupied. The section, however, (as amended by the Deserted Tenements Act 1817) only applies where the premises were let at a rack rent or at a rent of three quarters of their yearly value and half a year's rent is in arrears, and where the tenant has deserted the premises and left them unoccupied 'so as no sufficient distress can be had to countervail the arrears of rent'. The landlord's application must be made to the local magistrates and two or more of them (or, in the Metropolitan Police District, a police constable: s13 of the Metropolitan Police Courts Act 1839) will then be obliged to visit the demised premises and affix a notice of a second visit to take place in not less than 14 days' time. If, on the second visit, the rent arrears have not been paid (or if there is no sufficient distress on the premises), the magistrates may give the landlord possession. There is no doubt that, in view of the cumbersome nature of this archaic procedure, the landlord's remedy of actual re-entry is to be preferred.

Alternatively, the landlord may have recourse, in certain circumstances, to s54 of the Landlord and Tenant Act 1954, but this provision is of limited application in the context of abandoned premises since it only applies where the landlord has power to give notice to quit and merely enables the court to terminate the tenancy despite the fact that such a notice cannot be served on the tenant.

7.7 Disclaimer of the lease

The insolvency of the tenant, whether an individual or a corporate body, provides a further possibility for the termination of the lease by virtue of disclaimer under ss172–182 (insolvent company) and ss306–317 (individual bankrupt) of the Insolvency Act 1986.

If either the landlord or tenant goes bankrupt, the tenancy will become vested in a trustee in bankruptcy. If the bankrupt's interest cannot be sold, or is likely to result in the bankrupt incurring further expense, the trustee in bankruptcy has the power (under s315 of the 1986 Act) to disclaim the tenancy. Similarly, in the case of a company, a liquidator may disclaim under s178 of the 1986 Act. Disclaimer operates so as to terminate the lease and all obligations between landlord and tenant: see further, Ch 6, at 6.6.

7.8 Exercise of an express power in the lease

A fixed term lease may entitle the landlord or tenant (or both) to determine the term early (prior to its expiry date) by means of an express power to determine. An option to determine (sometimes referred to as a break-clause) must be exercised strictly within any time limits laid down for its exercise, otherwise it is not ordinarily exercisable. Many commercial leases entitle the landlord to break the term for redevelopment or reconstruction of the demised premises. A break-clause may also be inserted so as to operate in conjunction with a rent review clause, allowing the landlord (or tenant) to break the lease if the reviewed rent is determined at below (or above) a certain stipulated figure.

In *Mannai Investment Co Ltd* v *Eagle Star Life Assurance Co Ltd* (1997), the lease provided that the tenant could determine the term by serving a notice of not less than six months expiring on the third anniversary of the commencement date of the term. The tenant served notice expiring on 12 January 1995. The landlord contended that the notice was invalid because the commencement date of the term was 13 January 1992. The House of Lords held that the proper test to be applied in determining the validity of the notice was whether it was obvious to a 'reasonable recipient' with knowledge of the terms of the lease (in particular, the third anniversary date) that the tenant wished to determine the lease on that date and not one day short.

Applying this test, the Court concluded that the landlord would not have been misled by the minor error in the notice.

Similarly, in *Garston* v *Scottish Widows' Fund and Life Assurance Society* (1998), a lease, dated 10 July 1985, was granted for a term of 20 years from 24 June 1985. Under a break clause, the tenant had the right to end the lease at the end of the tenth year (ie on 24 June 1995). By an error, the tenant's notice purported to end the lease on 9 July 1995. A moment's reflection would have indicated to the landlord (as a reasonable recipient of the notice) that the tenant intended to end the lease at the end of the tenth year but had confused the date of the lease with the date fixed for the commencement of the term. The notice was, therefore, held to be valid.

By contrast, in *Lemmerbell Ltd* v *Britannia LAS Direct Ltd* (1998), the Court of Appeal, applying the *Mannai* test, held that the tenant's break notice was defective. Here, by two leases dated 18 October 1990, the tenants, then known as *LAS Direct Ltd (Direct)*, held two separate premises from F, each containing a break clause enabling the tenants to determine the respective terms on 28 September 1995 upon giving six months' written notice to the landlord. In 1992, solicitors acting for *Direct* informed the landlords' solicitors that they acted for the *Life Association of Scotland (Life)*. It was also explained that *Life* and *Direct* were wholly owned subsidiaries of *LAS Holdings Ltd*. No request for consent to an assignment was made and no assignment took place. On 7 October 1994, two purported break notices were sent on behalf of 'the Life Association of Scotland Ltd successors in title to Direct' determining each lease on 28 September 1995. The Court of Appeal concluded that there was insufficient material from which it could be inferred that *Life* was the general agent of *Direct* with authority to give break notices. The defects in the notices could not, therefore, be cured by the application of the *Mannai* ruling. On an objective analysis, the reasonable recipient of the notices could not know, in the absence of evidence of an assignment, whether *Life* was the tenant (as stated in the notices) or not. It was, accordingly, impossible to cure the defect.

It is evident from this latest Court of Appeal decision that the *Mannai* test will not avail every party who has served a defective break notice. In *Lemmerbell*, it was by no means obvious that there was an error in the name of the tenant in the notices, nor who the actual tenants were, nor whether the sender of the notices was an authorised agent of the tenant. The moral of the case is that minor errors may be excused but substantive defects remain incurable.

7.9 Frustration

A lease is capable of being discharged by a frustrating event. In *National Carriers Ltd* v *Panalpina (Northern) Ltd* (1981), a warehouse was demised to the tenants for a term of 10 years from 1 January 1974. The only vehicular access to the warehouse was by a street which the local authority closed on 16 May 1979 because of the dangerous condition of a derelict warehouse nearby. The road was closed for 20 months, during which time the tenants' warehouse was rendered useless. In an action by the landlords for the recovery of unpaid rent, the tenants claimed that the lease had been frustrated. The House of Lords, although recognising that the doctrine of frustration was, in principle, applicable to leases, held on the facts that the lease had not been discharged by frustration. The tenants had only lost less than two years of use of the premises out of a total of 10 years. Moreover, the lease would still have nearly three years left to run after the interruption had ceased.

The actual circumstances in which a lease will become frustrated are likely to be rare. The House of Lords in *Panalpina* gave little guidance on this issue. It may be said, however, that if the event is so serious that it goes to the whole foundation of the lease, rendering the leasehold estate worthless and useless, it will amount to frustration (eg total destruction of the subject-matter of the lease by fire).

It is also possible for a party to the lease to be temporarily excused from the performance of a covenant on the grounds of impossibility or illegality. In contrast to a frustrating event (which automatically discharges the lease for ever), an event giving rise to frustratory mitigation merely *suspends* the performance of the obligation until such time as it can be performed or it becomes evident that performance will never be possible and it is properly frustrated: *John Lewis Properties plc* v *Viscount Chelsea* (1993), involving a building covenant. For the principle to apply, however, the change of circumstances must be outside the parties' control and beyond the parties' contemplation when they entered into the lease.

7.10 Acceptance of a repudiatory breach

It is now well established that a lease can be brought to an end by the acceptance of a repudiatory breach. The leading case, until recently, has been *Hussein* v *Mehlman* (1992) where the landlord granted the tenants a three-year assured shorthold tenancy of a house, subject to certain implied covenants to repair. From the commencement of the tenancy, the tenants complained to the landlord about the disrepair of the property. Eventually, one of the bedrooms was rendered uninhabitable by a ceiling collapse and the sitting room let in water and part of its ceiling bulged seriously. The landlord refused to carry out any repairs and the tenants returned the keys and vacated the house. The Court held that the landlord had been guilty of a repudiatory breach (in so far as the defects in the ceilings were such as to render the house as a whole unfit to be lived in) and the tenants, by vacating the premises and returning the keys, had accepted that repudiation as putting to an end to the tenancy.

The decision in *Mehlman* was treated as apparently correct, without argument, by the Court of Appeal in *Chartered Trust plc* v *Davies* (1997), who held that the landlords had been guilty of a repudiatory breach in letting adjacent premises to a pawnbroker in derogation from grant. The landlord's conduct had rendered the tenant virtually bankrupt as a result of the commercial sterilisation of her shop.

It is evident that, before a breach can be characterised as repudiatory, it must deprive the tenant of substantially the whole of his bargain, just as a supervening event must substantially deprive the tenant of the whole benefit of the contract before it can be said to frustrate the lease (see 7.9). In both *Hussein* and *Chartered Trust*, the tenant was deprived of substantially the whole of his bargain because, in the former, the tenant could not live there for the remainder of the term, and in the latter, her business had been effectively destroyed. By contrast, in *Nynehead Developments Ltd* v *RH Fibreboard Containers Ltd* (1999), the Court held that the breaches were not sufficiently fundamental to justify termination of the lease. In this case, involving commercial premises on an industrial estate, the lease granted the tenants the exclusive right to park vehicles on the forecourt for the purpose of loading and unloading. The landlords subsequently let two other units to other tenants who, in breach of their leases, continually parked their vehicles on the forecourt causing annoyance to the tenants. Eventually, the tenants vacated the premises and withheld rent. The landlords then issued proceedings claiming the arrears and, by way of defence, the tenants argued that that the landlords were in repudiatory breach in authorising and encouraging the commission of the nuisance, and that such repudiation had been accepted bringing the lease to an end. In holding that the breach was not repudiatory, the Court concluded that the unjustified parking was merely an irritant and a minor interference with the tenants' business activities.

Although the decision in *Nynehead* clarifies what constitutes a repudiatory breach in the leasehold context, a number of thorny issues remain unresolved. First, a difficulty relates to the legal consequences of contractual termination. Does acceptance of a repudiatory breach (or frustration, see 7.9 and 7.10) automatically discharge the lease? If not, what is the interrelation of these contractual doctrines and the provisions for termination of a business tenancy under Part II of the Landlord and Tenant Act 1954? The problem here is that commercial (and residential) tenancies are regulated by statute which may, depending on the wording of the statute, limit or impede the ability of the tenant (or, more significantly, the landlord) to apply contractual remedies in the leasehold context: see further, M Pawlowski, 'Contractual Termination of Leases – Unresolved Issues', *Property Law*, 7 September 1998, No 13, at pp 4–6. Secondly, are these contractual doctrines limited to the original parties to the lease? Or do they apply also as between say, original landlord and assignee of the lease? In the absence of privity of contract between these latter parties, the answer appears to be negative unless it can be argued that the assignee stands in the shoes of the assignor for this purpose. Thirdly, assuming the landlord has committed a repudiatory breach, does this entitle the tenant to claim loss of bargain damages for the loss of his lease? Presumably, it would be open to a business tenant to claim loss of profits (see eg *Rolph* v *Crouch* (1867)) and loss of goodwill and any diminution in the value of stock in trade.

7.11 Parties' rights on termination

7.11.1 *Landlord's remedies where tenant holds over*

Where a tenant holds over at the expiry of his fixed term, several possibilities may arise. The tenant may hold over as a periodic tenant by implication of law if rent is tendered and accepted by reference to some period, or he may have statutory rights of continuation (see automatic continuance, at 8.3), or the tenant may simply remain in possession with the landlord's consent as a tenant at will (see 1.4), or without the landlord's consent or objection as a tenant at sufferance (see 1.4). Where the tenant remains in occupation either as a tenant at will or at sufferance, in the absence of anything expressly agreed between the parties to the contrary, he will be obliged to pay the landlord a reasonable sum for such use and occupation. This is to be contrasted with a claim for mesne profits which have accrued from the date on which the lease ended until the date when possession is delivered up by the tenant. Aclaim for mesne profits is essentially an action for damages so as to compensate the landlord for his lost possession. It is only appropriate in cases where the tenant's occupation is no longer lawful (ie where he is a trespasser following the expiry of his lease). Often the rent paid immediately prior to termination is evidence of the value of the premises, but this is not necessarily conclusive. It is always open to the landlord to adduce valuation evidence of the actual value of the premises at the hearing of his action for possession.

If the tenant refuses to deliver up possession after the expiry of the term, the landlord may bring an action against the tenant for double the yearly value of the premises under s1 of the Landlord and Tenant Act 1730. In order to do this, however, the landlord must give the tenant notice of such a claim either before the expiration of the term or thereafter. The Act applies to yearly tenancies. Alternatively, where a tenant gives a notice to quit seeking to determine a tenancy and, despite the giving of the notice, wilfully or otherwise holds over after such a notice has expired, the landlord may bring an action for double rent under s18 of the Distress for Rent Act 1737: *Oliver Ashworth (Holdings) Ltd* v *Ballard (Kent) Ltd* (1999).

7.11.2 *Tenant's rights to fixtures and compensation*

(a) *Fixtures*

The term 'fixture' is the name applied to anything which has become so attached to the land as to form in law part of it. In determining whether an object has become a fixture, the two main factors which the court will consider are (a) the degree of annexation and (b) the purpose of the annexation. Under the degree of annexation test, a built-in bookcase would be classified as a fixture, but a bookcase attached to the wall with just two screws (so that it will not tip forward) would not. The question here is: how firmly fixed is the article to the land? Under the purpose of annexation test, the question is whether the article is fixed to make the article a better article or to make the land a permanently better land. Thus, for example, a tapestry attached by tacks to wooden strips nailed to the wall would not be a fixture for it is mounted simply to display it better as an article and not to make a permanent improvement to the premises. By contrast, stone ornaments forming part of an architectural design or layout in a garden will be fixtures and form part of the property.

If, according to the 'degree and purpose of annexation' test, an article is not a fixture, it may be removed by the person bringing it onto the land, or by his successors in title. This applies to tenants of demised land. If, however, the article is deemed a fixture, it cannot, generally speaking, be removed from the land and must be left for the owner on the basis that it has become part of the land. There are, however, three exceptions:

- domestic and ornamental fixtures;
- trade fixtures; and
- agricultural fixtures.

Such fixtures are deemed 'tenant's fixtures' and the tenant is entitled to remove them within a reasonable period of time and must make good any damage caused by their removal.

(b) *Compensation*

A business tenant is entitled, in certain circumstances, to compensation for disturbance and improvements upon quitting the holding: see further, Ch 8, at 8.6.

Chapter 8

Statutory Protection

8.1 Introduction

Most business tenants have the benefit of two quite distinct statutory codes:

- Part II of the Landlord and Tenant Act 1954 (as amended by the Law of Property Act 1969) which affords (a) security of tenure and (b) compensation for disturbance in certain cases where the landlord is entitled to possession;
- The Landlord and Tenant Act 1927 (as amended by the 1954 Act) which entitles the tenant to compensation for certain improvements upon leaving the premises.

The machinery contained in Part II of the 1954 Act comprises a complicated structure of notices and counter-notices which must be served by either the landlord or the tenant in order to bring about the effective termination or renewal of a commercial lease. The Act leaves the parties free to agree extensions and renewals and imposes no restrictions on the level of rents. Accordingly, the statutory provisions are of no immediate importance to the parties unless and until either the landlord is opposed to a renewal of the lease or negotiations for a renewal break down. In the former case, the landlord will normally take the initiative by serving a notice of termination under s25 of the Act. In the latter case, the deadlock could be broken by either:

- The landlord serving a s25 notice stating that he would oppose an application for a new tenancy; or
- The tenant serving a request for a new tenancy under s26.

Given that a business tenancy continues under Part II on the same terms as originally granted, it is usual for the landlord to take the initiative under s25. It would, however, be otherwise if the tenant wished to regularise his position (eg before selling his business).

8.2 Application of Part II

In order to qualify as a business tenancy within Part II, the tenancy must fall within the requirements of s23 of the 1954 Act. In addition, it must not form an excluded tenancy within the meaning of s43.

8.2.1 Requirements of s23(1)

Section 23(1) provides that:

> ...this Part of this Act applies to any **tenancy** where the property comprised in the tenancy is or includes **premises** which are occupied by the tenant and are so **occupied for the purposes of a business** carried on by him or for those and other purposes. (Emphasis added).

Since s23(1) talks in terms of a 'tenancy', it is evident that licences are, by implication, excluded from the operation of Part II. The test for determining whether a particular occupancy constitutes a tenancy or a licence in the commercial context is the same as that for residential tenancies: see earlier *Street* v *Mountford* (1985), Ch 1, at 1.2.6. It is also possible to grant a trade concession without creating a tenancy: *Crane* v *Morris* (1965). In view, however, of the potential likelihood of a licence agreement being construed by the courts as a tenancy (within Part II), the better course is to contract out of Part II by an agreement sanctioned by the court under s38(4)(a) of the 1954 Act (see 8.2.2).

The expression 'premises' in s23(1) has been broadly construed to include land even though no buildings are standing on it. Thus, it is possible for a vacant plot used for car parking to constitute premises for the purpose of Part II.

Section 23(1) also requires that the premises be 'occupied by the tenant ... for the puposes of a business'. The Act draws a sharp distinction between individuals, on the one hand, who must be engaged in a trade, profession or employment, and bodies of persons (eg clubs, partnerships, companies) on the other, where 'any activity' suffices: see s23(2). It seems, however, that, although the activity need not strictly be a trade, profession or employment, nevertheless it must be something which is correlative to the conceptions involved in those words. In *Hillil Property & Investment Co Ltd* v *Naraine Pharmacy Ltd* (1979), a company tenant which used premises simply for dumping waste building materials from another property was held not to be indulging in an 'activity' within s23(2).

A tenant occupying a building for the sole purpose of sub-letting parts falls outside s23(1). In *Graysim Holdings Ltd* v *P & O Property Holdings Ltd* (1996), the House of Lords held that intermediate landlords who are not themselves in actual physical occupation of the premises are not within the class of persons protected by Part II, which is concerned to protect tenants in their occupation of property for the purpose of their business, not to give protection to tenants in respect of income from sublettings. Moreover, Part II makes no provision for 'dual occupation' of premises. In other words, it looks through a sub-letting to the occupying tenant and affords him statutory protection, not the landlord. It is important, however, to bear in mind that the House of Lords did not rule out the possibility that, in exceptional cases, the rights reserved by the tenant might be so extensive that he would remain in occupation of the property for the purposes of Part II: see *Lee-Verhulst (Investments) Ltd* v *Harwood Trust* (1973), where the sub-lettings comprised furnished rooms with substantial services (ie supply of blankets, bed linen and towels, daily cleaning of rooms, regular change of linen and provision of light meals if required): see further Ch 1, at 1.2.6.

In most cases, the tenant will be in personal occupation of the premises, but it is also possible for a tenant to occupy through his employee, manager or other agent.

8.2.2 Excluded tenancies

A number of tenancies are expressly excluded from Part II under s43 of the 1954 Act. It is possible, for example, to exclude the operation of Part II by granting a fixed term for not more than six months (s43(3)). The exclusion does not, however, apply, (a) where there is provision in the lease for renewal or extension beyond six months from the beginning of the tenancy or (b) where the tenant has already been in occupation for a period which, together with any period of occupation by a predecessor in the same business, exceeds 12 months. The practical difficulty of adopting this device as a method of avoiding security under Part II is that it may prove difficult for a landlord to find a potential tenant willing to enter into a tenancy for such a short duration.

A tenancy at will created by express agreement (or by operation of law) also falls outside the scope of Part II: see *Hagee (London) Ltd* v *AB Erikson and Larson* (1976). A tenancy at will exists where the premises are occupied 'at the will' of the landlord (ie with the latter's consent) but for an uncertain period. It may be terminated at any time by a demand for possession. If possession is demanded, the tenant must leave immediately.

In addition, the procedure under s38(4) provides the landlord with a useful mechanism for contracting out of security under Part II. This involves a joint application (by prospective landlord and tenant) to court for approval of an agreement excluding the principal provisions (sections 24–28) of the 1954 Act. Invariably the court will grant the order under a joint application, especially where there is clear evidence that both parties have taken independent legal advice. It is also important for·the application to set out the reasons why both landlord and tenant do not wish the provisions of Part II to apply to the tenancy (eg because the tenant is waiting to relocate to bigger premises once they are ready for occupation or the landlord requires the premises for development in the near future).

8.3 Automatic continuance and non-statutory methods of termination

Under s24(1) of the 1954 Act, a tenancy to which Part II of the 1954 Act applies cannot come to an end except in the manner provided by the Act. The most important effects are that a fixed-term continues after its contractual expiry date and a periodic tenancy cannot be determined by a normal notice to quit.

Quite apart from the statutory methods of termination (discussed in 8.4), a business tenancy can come to an end in the following ways:

• By notice to quit given by the tenant. But a notice given before the tenant has been in occupation as tenant for one month is invalid. A tenant for a fixed term who desires to vacate may prevent continuance by giving written notice to his immediate landlord not later than three months before the expiry date of the tenancy: s27(1). Thereafter, he must give not less than three months' notice to terminate on any quarter day: s27(2). The right of a periodic tenant to give a notice to quit in the normal way is preserved by s24;

• By surrender of the tenancy, provided that the instrument of surrender was not executed before (or executed in pursuance of) any agreement to surrender concluded before the tenant had been in occupation for one month;

- By forfeiture of the tenancy (or a superior tenancy) by the landlord for breach of the tenant's covenants or his insolvency;
- On the tenancy ceasing to be one to which Part II applies. Thus, if the tenant ceases to occupy for the purposes of his business at the expiry of a fixed term, there can be no continuance under s24: see *Esselte AB* v *Pearl Assurance plc* (1997). At the expiry of the contractual term, the tenant has the option either to remain in occupation of the premises or simply vacate without any prior notice to the landlord. If the tenant leaves, Part II will not extend the tenant's liability (eg for rent) beyond the term date. The tenant may (but is not obliged to) formalise the position by serving notice under s27(1) (see above). If the tenant ceases to occupy *after* expiry of a fixed term, the tenancy does not end for that reason alone and the tenant must serve a s27(2) notice on the landlord to bring the tenancy to an end. In this context, the *Esselte* decision has no application since the 1954 Act draws a clear distinction between the period before expiry of the contractual term and the period after expiry. A landlord may also terminate the tenancy in these circumstances by giving minimum three, maximum six months' notice in writing to the tenant: s24(3)(a). (If the tenant ceases to occupy during a *periodic* tenancy, it seems that the landlord's ability to serve an effective common law notice revives);
- By agreement for a new tenancy, under which the old tenancy ceases to be subject to the Act on the date agreed for the new tenancy provided that the new tenancy comprises the same holding: s28.

A business tenancy which is continued by the 1954 Act can be assigned and is transmitted on death and bankruptcy in the normal way. The terms of the contractual tenancy (eg rent, repairs, forfeiture) continue to apply. The only feature which is changed is the mode of termination. The continuation tenancy can only be terminated in accordance with the statutory machinery for termination prescribed by the Act (see 8.4 below).

8.4 Statutory machinery for termination/renewal

8.4.1 Introduction

The statutory machinery contained in Part II is complex. A landlord who desires possession must establish one or more specific grounds (listed in s30) having made a formal statement of the grounds relied on *either* by notice of termination complying with s25 *or* by a notice of opposition to a tenant's request for a new tenancy under s26. A tenant who wishes to renew his business tenancy must apply for renewal *either* pursuant to a request for a new tenancy under s26 *or* pursuant to a counter-notice in response to a landlord's notice of termination served under s25: see chart below outlining the procedure for both landlord and tenant.

In order to comply with the requirements of the Act, both parties may need information as to the interests existing in the demised property. For example, the tenant will need to know who is the competent landlord, and the landlord may wish to identify who is currently occupying the premises (ie the tenant or a subtenant). Such information may be obtained by making use of the procedures laid down in s40 of the 1954 Act. The landlord can serve notice on the tenant requiring him to notify the landlord within a month of the position regarding the occupation of the premises, and of the existence and terms of any subtenancies: s40(2). Equally, the tenant can require information from anyone holding a superior interest in the property as to the ownership of the freehold, the identity of the superior landlord, and the duration of his interest: s40(3). There are, however, no penalties for failing to comply with such requests for information.

8.4.2 Requirements for effective s25 notice of termination

In order to trigger the statutory machinery for termination, the landlord is obliged to serve a notice of termination upon his business tenant in accordance with s25. The notice must be in the presecribed form or substantially to the like effect. The notice must be given not more than 12 months and not less than six months before the termination date specified in the notice, which date must not be earlier than the date at which the tenancy would expire or could be brought to an end by the landlord at common law. For this purpose, tenancies are divided into two broad categories:

- Periodic tenancies which, apart from the Act, could have been brought to an end by notice to quit, when the specified date must not be earlier than the earliest date on which the tenancy could have been so terminated; and
- Any other tenancy, including a fixed term, where the specified date must not be earlier than the date when the tenancy would have come to an end by effluxion of time.

In addition to the above, the landlord's notice must require the tenant to notify the landlord in writing within two months whether or not the tenant will be willing to give up possession at the date specified in the notice and must state whether the landlord would oppose a tenant's application to the court for a new tenancy and, if so, on which of the seven grounds specified in s30(1) of the 1954 Act (see 8.4.8 below). It is important to bear in mind that there is no provision in the Act (or elsewhere) for the amendment of a landlord's notice and, accordingly, a landlord cannot depart from the grounds of opposition stated in the notice. (Conversely, however, a landlord's successors may adopt the grounds stated in the notice). Furthermore, the withdrawal of a notice with a view to serving a fresh notice stating different grounds seems to be excluded by s24(1) of the Act, although there is no direct authority on this point.

In the light of the foregoing, a careful statement of the grounds relied upon by the landlord is, clearly, advisable notwithstanding that minor slips are excusable by the courts provided that the tenant has a fair warning of the case he has to answer: *Carradine Properties Ltd* v *Aslam* (1976).

8.4.3 Tenant's counter-notice

There is no prescribed form for the tenant's counter-notice under the 1954 Act and, accordingly, a simple letter notifying the landlord whether or not the tenant will be willing to give up possession at the date specified in the notice will suffice. The tenant's counter-notice must, of course, be served within two months of the landlord giving notice under s25 as a condition precedent to the tenant's application for a new tenancy under s24. Moreover, a counter-notice that expresses *willingness* to give up possession once served is irrevocable: *Re 14 Grafton Street, London W1* (1971).

8.4.4 Requirements for effective s26 request for a new tenancy

Not all business tenants are given the right to serve a request under the 1954 Act. Only those tenants whose current tenancy was granted for *either* a term of years certain exceeding one year (whether or not continued under s24) *or* a term of years certain and thereafter from year to year are given this privilege. It is evident, therefore, that

Statutory Machinery for Termination
Outline of Procedure

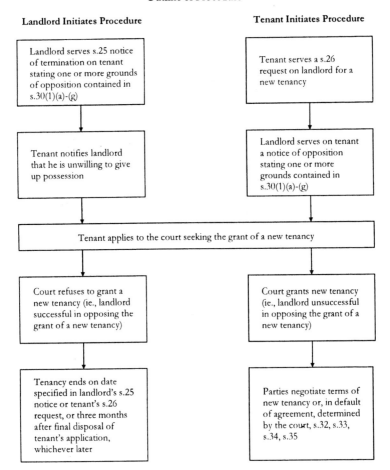

Landlord Initiates Procedure

Landlord serves s.25 notice of termination on tenant stating one or more grounds of opposition contained in s.30(1)(a)-(g)

Tenant notifies landlord that he is unwilling to give up possession

Tenant Initiates Procedure

Tenant serves a s.26 request on landlord for a new tenancy

Landlord serves on tenant a notice of opposition stating one or more grounds contained in s.30(1)(a)-(g)

Tenant applies to the court seeking the grant of a new tenancy

Court refuses to grant a new tenancy (ie., landlord successful in opposing the grant of a new tenancy)

Court grants new tenancy (ie., landlord unsuccessful in opposing the grant of a new tenancy)

Tenancy ends on date specified in landlord's s.25 notice or tenant's s.26 request, or three months after final disposal of tenant's application, whichever later

Parties negotiate terms of new tenancy or, in default of agreement, determined by the court, s.32, s.33, s.34, s.35

yearly and other forms of periodic tenancies and fixed-term tenancies of less than one year fall outside s26, although this does not mean that tenants falling within this category are without protection under Part II, since they continue to be entitled to serve a counter-notice in response to a landlord's notice of termination and to apply for a new tenancy. The Act merely prohibits these categories of tenant from initiating the renewal machinery in the first instance.

The tenant's request must be for a tenancy commencing (a) not more than 12 and not less than six months after making the request and (b) not earlier than the expiry date of the current tenancy or the earliest date on which the current tenancy could be brought to an end by notice to quit given by the tenant. Furthermore, the request must be in the prescribed form and set out the tenant's proposals as to the terms of the new tenancy (ie as to the property comprised in the tenancy, rent and duration of term).

The machinery of Part II does not permit the making of a request after the landlord has served a s25 notice of termination or after the tenant has served a notice to quit under s27 of the Act (see 8.1 and 8.3 earlier). The effect of the request is essentially twofold:

- To give the landlord two months within which to serve a notice of opposition to any application for any new tenancy on one or more of the grounds specified in s30(1)(a) to (g); and
- To give the tenant the right to apply for a new tenancy within certain specified time-limits, failing which his tenancy terminates on the day before the date specified in the request.

8.4.5 Service of notices

For the purpose of Part II, the various notices referred to above are served between 'the competent landlord' (being either freeholder or, where there is a mesne landlord(s) and sub-tenant(s), the first landlord up the ladder of tenancies whose interest will not expire within 14 months or less by effluxion of time) and the occupying business tenant.

Section 23 of the Landlord and Tenant Act 1927 provides that any notice or request under the 1954 Act is to be served either personally or by leaving it at the last known place of abode in England and Wales of the person to be served or by sending it through the post in a registered letter addressed to him there and, in the case of a notice to a landlord, his duly authorised agent. The phrase 'place of abode' in s23 is not confined to the residence of the person concerned but will include his business address.

Notices can be sent by the ordinary post, but it is preferable to use the recorded delivery service, which can also be used as an alternative to the registered post: see the Recorded Delivery Service Act 1962. It should also be noted that if the registered or recorded delivery post is used, the presumption of delivery cannot be rebutted, whereas this is not the case if the ordinary post is used.

8.4.6 *Waiver of notices*

It is clear that a party may be estopped (ie prevented) from denying
the validity of a notice. For example, in *Bristol Cars Ltd v RKH
(Hotels) Ltd* (1979), the tenant gave a notice requesting a new
tenancy under s26, but the notice was defective because the date of
commencement was too early to be capable of inclusion in the
notice. Neither party noticed the mistake. The landlords indicated
that they would not oppose the new tenancy but later were advised
that the tenant's request was bad and they applied for the tenant's
application to be struck out. The Court of Appeal held that the
landlords were estopped by their conduct from denying the
validity of the tenant's request and, alternatively, their application
for an interim rent (which was ultimately not pursued) amounted
to a waiver of any defect in the tenant's notice.

8.4.7 *Tenant's application for a new tenancy*

The tenant's right to apply for a new tenancy depends on the
fulfilment of the following conditions:

- The service of a s25 notice or s26 request on the part of the tenant
  or landlord, respectively;
- The tenant must have served a counter-notice notifying the
  landlord within two months that he was not willing to give up
  possession (where the application is consequent upon a s25
  notice);
- The application itself must be made not less than two months
  and not more than four months after the giving of the s25 notice
  or s26 request, as the case may be.

A business tenant who, having requested a new tenancy, fails to
apply to the court for such new tenancy within the time-limits
provided by the Act, cannot later make such an application out of
time. The court does, however, have power to enlarge the time
available for service of a tenant's application. An application for a
new tenancy made out of time is, nevertheless, 'an application'
within the meaning of the 1954 Act, so that the tenancy will
continue until three months after proceedings are finally disposed
of: see s64 of the 1954 Act and *Zenith Investments (Torquay) Ltd v
Kammins Ballrooms Co Ltd (No 2)* (1971).

As with notices and requests, the time-limit imposed under the
Act in respect of the tenant's application to the court is capable of

waiver by the landlord: *Kammins Ballrooms Co Ltd* v *Zenith Investments (Torquay) Ltd* (1971), where on the facts the landlords were held not to have waived their right to object that the application was bad merely by filing a reply to a premature application.

The tenant must, of course, commence his application against the person who is the 'competent landlord' for the time being (see 8.4.5 earlier) and, therefore, if the respondent to the tenant's application ceases to be the competent landlord after proceedings are commenced, the new competent landlord must be joined as a party.

8.4.8 *Landlord's opposition to a new tenancy*

The landlord may oppose a tenant's application for a new tenancy by invoking one or more of the seven grounds of oppostion listed in s30(1)(a) to (g) of the 1954 Act, provided that these have been stated in his s25 notice or notice of opposition to a tenant's request under s26 (see 8.4.2 above).

The grounds of opposition under paragraphs (e), (f) or (g) must be established with reference to 'the holding'. This is defined in s23(3) to mean the property comprised in the tenancy, but excluding any part which is occupied neither by the tenant nor by any person employed by the tenant for the purposes of the tenant's business.

It is common practice for the validity of the landlord's grounds of opposition to be determined in court as a preliminary issue in order to save time and expense. If the landlord takes this course and objects successfully, he will save himself the expense of preparing a case for disputing the terms of a new tenancy (see 8.5). The grounds of opposition are as follows:

- Tenant has failed to repair the holding: s30(1)(a). Proof of a breach of covenant, although essential, is not enough. The landlord must show that the state of disrepair of the holding at the date of the hearing is such that a new tenancy 'ought not to be granted'. Accordingly, the court has a broad discretion whether or not to grant a new tenancy;
- Tenant has persistently delayed in paying rent: s30(1)(b). The landlord must show that a new tenancy ought not to be granted in view of the delay in paying rent. Thus, if the reason for the delay has ceased to apply, the landlord might fail under this ground;
- Tenant has committed substantial breaches of obligations under the tenancy or there are other reasons connected with the use or

management of the holding: s30(1)(c). Once again, the landlord must show that a new tenancy ought not to be granted in view of the tenant's breaches or other reasons;

- Landlord has offered alternative accommodation: s30(1)(d). The accommodation must be (a) provided or secured by the landlord and (b) a reasonable alternative to the holding in all respects including the preservation of goodwill;
- Landlord would obtain a better return if the holding was let or sold as part of a larger unit: s30(1)(e). This ground is not available to an immediate landlord of the applicant and is only established where: (a) the relationship between the competent landlord and the applicant is that of superior landlord and sub-tenant; (b) the sub-tenancy comprises only part of the property comprised in the superior tenancy; (c) the total rent obtainable on separate lettings of the holding and the rest of the letting of the property (comprised in the superior letting) would be substantially less than on the letting of the property as a whole; and (d) on termination of the applicant's current tenancy, the landlord requires possession of the holding for the purpose of letting or otherwise disposing of the property as a whole;
- Landlord intends to demolish or reconstruct or effect substantial work of construction: s30(1)(f). The landlord's intention must exist at the time of the hearing but it is immaterial that the landlord's s25 notice was served by a predecessor who had no such intention. Bare assertions of intention are not enough and the landlord will fail if serious difficulties (eg obtaining planning permission or finance) lie ahead. A formal resolution expressing an intention to develop is not essential to establish the existence of that intention by a body corporate: *Poppets (Caterers) Ltd v Maidenhead Corporation* (1971), where no formal resolution was passed but the development was approved in principle in committee and noted in the committee's minutes. The landlord's intention must be to effect the work on termination of the current tenancy. His motive for effecting the intended work is immaterial (eg that he intends to occupy the rebuilt premises himself), nor is the intended method of carrying out the work relevant (eg by means of a building lease). In addition to establishing the requisite intention, the landlord must show that he requires legal possession of the holding. As a general rule, this is satisfied where he shows that the work could not be done satisfactorily unless he obtains exclusive occupation of the holding. Thus, the landlord will fail if the tenancy contains an access clause and the

proposed work falls within the terms of that clause. Moreover, the tenant may be able to rely upon the provisions of s31Aof the 1954 Act (added by the Law of Property Act 1969) to resist the landlord's claim for possession of the holding. Under this section, the landlord will fail to establish the need for legal possession of the holding if (a) the tenant agrees to the inclusion in the new tenancy terms giving the landlord access and other facilities for carrying out the work and, given such access, the landlord can reasonably carry out the work without interfering for a substantial time or extent with the tenant's business or (b) the tenant is willing to accept a tenancy of an 'economically separable' part of the holding (with or without access terms) and the landlord can carry out the work by virtue of this reduction. Section 31A, however, does not give the court power to limit the work the landlord intends to carry out;

- The landlord intends to occupy the holding for the purpose of a business to be carried on by him, or as his residence: s30(1)(g). In deciding whether a landlord intends to occupy the holding himself, not only must he have a genuine *bona fide* intention to do so but he must also, on an objective test, have a reasonable prospect of bringing about this occupation by his own act or volition: *Gregson* v *Cyril Lord Ltd* (1963). The wisdom or long term viability of the landlord's proposed business are irrelevant in determining the requisite intention under s30(1)(g). Moreover, the absence of detailed plans, permissions and consents will also not necessarily denote lack of intention. The crucial factor in all cases is the reality of the landlord's intention to start the proposed business, not the probability of its achieving its start, or even less, its ultimate success: see *Dolgellau Golf Club* v *Hett* (1998), illustrating a judicial trend towards a less restrictive approach with regard to the interpretation of ground (g) which, no doubt, will make it easier for landlords to claim possession against their business tenants. The general rule is that the intended business must be the landlord's business, but it is sufficient if the landlord intends to occupy and carry on the business through an agent or manager. Moreover, by way of statutory exception, it is enough if the landlord has a controlling interest in a company and it is intended that the company will occupy (s30(3)), or where the landlord is a company and the business is to be carried on by another company in the same group (s42(3)). It should be noted that ground (g) is excluded altogether where the landlord's interest in the premises was purchased or created during the period of five years ending with the termination of the tenancy: s30(2).

If the landlord, having relied on grounds (d), (e) or (f), fails to establish those grounds but satisfies the court that he would have been successful if the date specified in his s25 notice (or tenant's s26 request) had been a later date (being not more than 12 months from the date actually specified), the court has jurisdiction to order that the later date be substituted for the date in the notice (or request): s31(2). Thus, if the landlord is initially unsuccessful in establishing the requisite intention to demolish or reconstruct the premises at the date of the hearing, it is still open to him to rely on s31(2) in order to gain possession at some date in the foreseeable future. Even if the landlord cannot bring his case within the near-miss provisions of s31(2) (because his intention to commence development extends beyond the 12-month requisite period), he may still argue that the court should grant a relatively short term bearing in mind that the premises may be ripe for development (see 8.5.3 later).

8.5 Terms of the new tenancy

8.5.1 Introduction

Given a successful application by the tenant, the court is bound to order the grant of a new tenancy: s29. However, the court may only determine the terms of the new tenancy in default of agreement between the parties. The limits set out below as to property, duration, rent and other terms apply only in so far as the parties have failed to agree on these matters.

8.5.2 Property

As a general rule, the grant must be of the holding as existing at the date of the order. This rule, however, is subject to two exceptions:

- Where the landlord has opposed on ground (f) of s30(1) and the court is empowered to grant part of the holding under s31A (see 8.4.8 above); and
- Where the landlord insists on the grant of the entire premises comprised in the current tenancy (s32(2)).

Unless the parties agree otherwise, the tenant is also entitled to the re-grant of any easements or profits enjoyed under the current tenancy.

8.5.3 *Duration*

The court is empowered to order such term as is reasonable subject to an upper-limit of 14 years: s33. The court has, for example, full discretion to order a short term where the landlord fails to establish grounds (d)–(g) of s30(1) but persuades the court that he is likely to be able to establish such grounds in the near future (see 8.4.8 above). The court may also grant a short term where the tenant requires only enough time to make an orderly departure from the premises with a view to moving to a new location.

Instead of granting a short term, the court may insert a break-clause allowing the landlord to determine the lease when ready to demolish or reconstruct the premises. The governing principle is that, if there is a real possibility that the premises will be required for redevelopment during the continuance of the proposed new tenancy, then a break-clause should be included in the terms of the new tenancy. Moreover, it is primarily a question of what the landlord *bona fide* wants to do with the property and not what is considered objectively to be ripe for development.

The grant of a new tenancy is governed by s64(1) of the 1954 Act so that a new tenancy does not commence until the expiration of a period of three months after the termination of all proceedings relating to the tenant's application.

8.5.4 *Rent*

Under s34, the rent to be determined is such rent, having regard to the terms of the tenancy (except rent) as the holding might reasonably be expected to be let in the open market by a willing lessor. However, the court must disregard:

- Such prestige (or adverse image) attaching to the holding as is attributable to occupation by the tenant or his predecessor in title;
- Goodwill attached to the holding by virtue of the business conducted by the tenant or a predecessor in business;
- Improvements which (a) were carried out by the tenant for the time being; (b) were not improvements which the tenant was bound to do; and (c) were *either* carried out during the current tenancy *or* carried out not earlier than 21 years before the date of the application *and* the part affected by the improvement has been at all times let on business tenancies none of which has been terminated by a tenant's notice to quit; and

- The value of any liquor licence held by the tenant.

The new rent will usually be determined by reference to comparable evidence but, where there are no suitable comparables, reference may be made to the general increase in rents in the area. The zoning method of valuation may also be appropriate in determining the new rent.

The court has power to determine a variable rent, increasing by fixed amounts at specific times and to insert a rent review clause in the new tenancy so as not to prejudice the landlord where a long term is granted. Moreover, the review clause may provide for a review of the rent downwards as well as upwards. The date from which the rent is to be determined is the date of the hearing, but taking account of matters which could reasonably be expected to happen between that date and the date of the commencement of the new term.

8.5.5 *Other terms*

Section 35 directs the court to have regard to the terms of the current tenancy and to all relevant circumstances in determining the other terms of the new tenancy. The landlord is not entitled without justification to the insertion of terms which are more onerous than the terms in the current tenancy.

8.6 Tenant's claim to compensation for disturbance and improvements

8.6.1 *Compensation for disturbance*

This form of compensation is available to the tenant where the landlord successfully objects to the grant of a new tenancy on grounds (e), (f) or (g) of s30(1): see s37(1). The compensation is recoverable from the landlord from the date that the tenant quits the holding.

The amount of compensation is equal to the rateable value of the holding at the date of the s25 notice or s26 request or double this amount where the tenant can show continuous occupation as a business tenant over a period of 14 years immediately preceding termination of the current tenancy. Personal occupation over the 14-year period is not, however, necessary where all the previous occupants were predecessors in the same business: s37(3).

Agreements restricting or excluding compensation are void except where, looking back from the date that the tenant quit the holding, there was less than five years' continuous business occupation by the tenant or his predecessors in business: s38. When determining whether the business tenant has occupied for the whole of the five-year period, the courts are reluctant to find that business occupancy has ceased where the business premises are empty for only a short period, whether mid-term or before or after trading at either end of the lease, provided always that during that period there existed no rival for the role of business occupant and that the premises were not being used for some other non-business purpose. However, if the premises are left vacant for a period of months, the courts are more likely to conclude that the reason for that period of closure was not an incident in the ordinary course or conduct of business life and that the 'thread of continuity' had been broken: *Bacchiocchi* v *Academic Agency Ltd* (1998), where the tenant was held to have been in business occupation despite the premises standing empty for 12 days prior to termination of the lease.

8.6.2 *Compensation for improvements*

A business tenant will often undertake improvements to the premises for which he may be entitled to compensation upon quitting the holding under Part I of the Landlord and Tenant Act 1927 (as amended by Part III of the Landlord and Tenant Act 1954). In order to be eligible for compensation, the tenant must have complied with the following pre-conditions:

• The tenant must show an improvement on his holding made by him or his predecessors in title. In order for an improvement to qualify, it must (a) be of such a nature as to be calculated to add to the letting value of the holding at the termination of the tenancy; (b) be reasonable and suitable to the character of the holding and (c) not diminish the value of any other property belonging to the same landlord or to any superior landlord from whom the immediate landlord of the tenant directly or indirectly holds;

• The tenant must have served on the landlord a notice of intention to effect the improvement prior to the commencement of the works. If the landlord makes no objection, the tenant may go ahead and carry out the works without recourse to litigation. If, however, the landlord, within three months after service of the tenant's notice, serves on the tenant a notice of objection to the proposed improvement, the tenant must then apply to the court for a certificate that the improvement is a proper one if he wishes to proceed with the works;

- The tenant must have completed the improvement within the time agreed with the landlord or fixed by the court. Once the tenant has executed the improvement, he is entitled to request the landlord to furnish him with a certificate that the improvement has been duly executed. If the landlord fails or refuses to do so (within one month of the tenant's request), the tenant can apply to the court for a certificate that the improvement has been duly executed;
- The tenant must give notice to the landlord of his claim for compensation within the time-limits specified in s47 of the 1954 Act.

The amount of compensation is fixed by agreement between the parties or, in default, by the court. Section 1(1) of the 1927 Act provides that the sum to be paid as compensation for any improvement shall not exceed:

- The net addition to the value of the holding as a whole which may be determined to be the direct result of the improvement; or
- The reasonable cost of carrying out the improvement at the termination of the tenancy, subject to a deduction of an amount equal to the cost (if any) of putting the works constituting the improvement into a reasonable state of repair, except so far as such cost is covered by the liability of the tenant under any covenant or agreement as to the repair of the premises.

8.7 Landlord's application for interim rent

Under s64 of the 1954 Act, once the tenant has applied for a new tenancy, the current tenancy cannot end earlier than three months after the date on which the tenant's application is 'finally disposed of'. If the tenant appeals, the application continues to be 'undisposed of'. Hence, a tenant paying a low rent under his current tenancy would have every incentive to drag his application out as long as possible.

Under s24A of the 1954 Act (added by the Law of Property Act 1969), the landlord may apply for the fixing of an interim rent as soon as a s25 notice or s26 request has been served. The rent so fixed becomes payable from the date specified in the notice/request or the date of the landlord's application under s24A, whichever is the later. Alternatively, the landlord may apply for an interim rent in his answer to an application by the tenant for a new tenancy, and any order for an interim rent will take effect from the date of the answer.

Although the power of the court to determine an interim rent is discretionary, the discretion is usually exercised in favour of determining such a rent in normal cases. Moreover, the landlord's application for an interim rent is not affected by the tenant's withdrawal of his application for a new tenancy since the former is not parasitic but a wholly distinct claim for independent relief.

As to the amount of interim rent, the court must apply the same criteria as laid down under s34 (see 8.5.4 above) for new tenancies but with the following modifications:

- The rent must be based on a notional tenancy from year to year;
- The court may consider the rent payable under the current tenancy. The ability to do this enables the court to 'cushion the blow' to the tenant by awarding less than the market rent under s24A. In some circumstances, the court has power to fix a differential rent pending completion of necessary repairs by the landlord.

For an interesting exposition of the relevant legal and valuation principles involved in determining an interim rent, see *Department of the Environment* v *Allied Freehold Property Trust* (1992).

Specimen Lease of Shop Premises

The specimen lease is reproduced for illustrative purposes only by kind permission of The Solicitor's Law Stationery Society Limited.

This Lease made the   day of

Between

(hereinafter called "the Lessor   " which expression where the context admits includes the persons for the time being entitled in reversion expectant on the term hereby granted) of the one part and

(hereinafter called "the Lessee   " which expression where the context admits includes the persons deriving title under the Lessee) of the other part

Witnesses as follows: ——

1. IN consideration of the rent hereinafter reserved and of the covenants by the Lessee hereinafter contained the Lessor   hereby demise[s] unto the Lessee

All that   shop or property known as

the site of which property is delineated on the plan hereto and thereon edged pink EXCEPT NEVERTHELESS out of this demise and reserved unto the Lessor   Full right of passage and running of water soil and electric current from all neighbouring lands and houses of the Lessor   through all drains channels pipes and sewers in and under the said property TO HOLD (except and reserved as aforesaid) unto the Lessee   from the
day of   for the
term of   years thence next
ensuing YIELDING AND PAYING therefor unto the Lessor   the yearly rent of £
(subject to review and variation as hereinafter provided) the rent to be paid clear of all deductions (except as hereinafter mentioned) by equal quarterly payments on the usual quarter-days in every year the first of such quarterly payments or a proper proportion thereof to be made on the   day of   next and the last to be made in advance on the quarter-day immediately preceding the expiration or earlier determination of the term.

2.   THE Lessee   hereby [jointly and severally] covenant[s] with the Lessor   :—

(1) During the term to pay the rent at the times and in manner aforesaid free from all deductions except as may be authorised by statute.

(2) To pay all rates taxes charges assessments and outgoings whether parliamentary parochial or otherwise which now are or which at any time hereafter shall be assessed or imposed in respect of the premises or on the owner or occupier thereof.

(3) At all times during the term at the Lessees own cost when and as often as need or occasion shall require well and substantially to repair amend renew uphold support maintain paint grain varnish paper whitewash and cleanse the premises and the drains sewers watercourses walls fences fixtures fittings and appurtenances belonging thereto And in particular to paint in a good and workmanlike manner twice over with paint of a good quality or otherwise suitably treat all the outside wood iron and other work of the premises (usually painted or treated) once in every   year during the term   And in like manner once in every   year of the term to paint with two coats of paint of a good quality and paper with suitable papers the internal wood metal and cement work which has been or ought to be painted or papered.

(4) At the end or other sooner determination of the term peaceably to surrender and yield up the premises (being so well and substantially repaired amended renewed   upheld supported maintained painted grained varnished papered whitewashed and cleansed as aforesaid) unto the Lessor   together with all fixtures which at any time during the term shall have been affixed or shall belong to the premises (tenant's and trade fixtures only excepted) and to replace all broken glass.

(5) To permit the Lessor   or any person authorised by the Lessor   (with or without surveyors agents workmen and others) during the term at reasonable hours in the daytime to enter into and upon the premises for the purposes of carrying out any of the responsibilities of the Lessor   under the Offices, Shops and Railway Premises Act 1963 or the Health and Safety at Work Act 1974 or regulations made thereunder or in order to view and examine the state and condition of the premises and so that if all defects decay or want of reparation or amendment which upon such view shall be found the Lessor may give or leave notice in writing at or upon the premises for the Lessee   to repair and amend the same.

(6) At the Lessees own expense within three months from the giving or leaving of such notice well and sufficiently to repair and amend the same accordingly.

(7) To keep use and occupy the shop for the trade or business of a only and not during the term to use exercise or carry on or permit or suffer to be used exercised or carried on in or upon the premises or any part thereof any other trade or business whatsoever or hold any sale by auction on the premises without obtaining the previous licence in writing of the Lessor

(8) Save in carrying out the responsibilities of the Lessee   under the Offices, Shops and Railway Premises Act 1963 or the Health and Safety at Work Act 1974 or regulations made thereunder not without the previous consent in writing of the Lessor   to make any alteration in or addition to the premises or erect any new building thereon.

(9) Not without the previous consent in writing of the Lessor   to carry out any operation or institute or continue any use of the premises for which planning permission   is required.

(10) Within seven days of receipt by the Lessee   of any notice order or proposal made given or issued by a planning authority under or by virtue of any enactment relating to town and country planning to give full particulars thereof to the Lessor   and also without delay to take all reasonable or necessary steps to comply with such notice   or order.

(11) Within seven days of the receipt by the Lessee   of any notice given under the Party Wall etc. Act 1996 to give full particulars thereof to the Lessor   and not without the agreement of the Lessor   (not to be unreasonably withheld) to consent to any works specified in any such notice or to serve a counter-notice in respect thereof Provided that if the Lessor   refuse   to agree that the Lessee   may consent to any such works   he   shall indemnify the Lessee   against any costs or expenses incurred by the Lessee   in consequence.

(12) Not to assign underlet charge or part with the possession of the premises or any part thereof without the consent in writing of the Lessor   provided that such consent shall not be unreasonably withheld but so that it is hereby agreed (for the   purposes also of section 19(1A) of the Landlord and Tenant Act 1927 if applicable) that   if the Lessor agrees to an assignment of the premises such consent may be given subject to the condition that the Lessee   shall enter into an authorised guarantee agreement within the meaning of the Landlord and Tenant (Covenants) Act 1995.

(13) (a) To insure and keep insured the premises from loss or damage by fire in   the Insurance   Office or with such insurers as the Lessor   may select in the joint names of the Lessor   and Lessee   in the sum of £   at least and to pay all premiums necessary for that purpose within seven days after the same become due.

(b) To produce the policy and the receipt for the current year's premium on such insurance whenever required to do so by the Lessor

(c) In case the premises or any part thereof shall be destroyed or damaged by fire with all convenient speed to lay out and expend the money to be received by virtue of any such insurance in or towards rebuilding or substantially repairing and reinstating the premises to the satisfaction of the Lessor   or the Lessors surveyor.

(d) In case the said money shall be insufficient for that purpose to make up the deficiency out of the Lessees own money.

(14) To pay the Lessor   all costs charges and expenses (including legal costs and fees payable to a surveyor) which may be incurred by the Lessor   in or in contemplation   of any proceedings under sections 146 and 147 of the Law of Property Act 1925.

(15) That the Lessor   or the Lessors agents shall have power at any time during the last three months before the expiration or sooner determination of the term to affix notices upon any conspicuous parts of the premises that the same are to be let or to be otherwise disposed of and also at all convenient hours in the daytime (by agents or otherwise) to enter upon and show the premises to any person.

3. FROM every review date (that is to say from the expiration of every year of the term) the rent may be reviewed and varied to the market rent of the premises and the following provisions shall apply —

(1) The machinery of review shall be a written notice given to the other party by the party requiring the review and (failing agreement on the amount of the new rent) the fixing of the new rent by an arbitrator agreed or (failing agreement on an arbitrator) appointed on the application of either party by the President of the Royal Institution of Chartered Surveyors.

(2) The "market rent" shall be the rent which having regard to the terms of the Lease (other than those relating to rent) the premises would at the review date currently command in the open market there being disregarded the several items mentioned in paragraphs (a) to (d) of section 34 of the Landlord and Tenant Act 1954 as amended by the Law of Property Act 1969.

(3) Time shall not in the first place be of the essence of the machinery of review but the time scale for notice requiring a review shall be three months (so that a three months or longer notice expiring on the review date shall always be effective) and either party may before or after the review date by writing require the other to serve notice or operate any other part of the machinery of review within a reasonable time (which shall become of the essence of the contract accordingly).

4. IF any part of the rent shall be in arrear for at least twenty-one days (whether or not lawfully demanded) or if there shall be a breach of any of the covenants by the Lessee herein contained the Lessor may re-enter upon the premises and immediately thereupon the term shall absolutely cease and determine but without prejudice to the other remedies of the Lessor .

5. THE Lessor hereby covenant[s] with the Lessee that the Lessee paying the rent and performing and observing all the covenants by the Lessee herein contained shall and may quietly hold and enjoy the premises during the term without any interruption by the Lessor or any person claiming through under or in trust for the Lessor

In Witness whereof the parties hereto have hereunto set their hands the day and year first above written.

Signed as a Deed and Delivered by the

in the presence of

Short-term Commercial Lease

How can commercial property transactions be made easier? While there is no one answer, the BPF is convinced that much could be achieved by the promotion of standard documents, widely recognised in the market as being fair and reasonable.

To start the process, the BPF has prepared a standard short-term commercial lease. Drafted following a wide-ranging consultation exercise, this consensus-based document has been designed to make life easier for landlords, tenants and their advisers. Written in plain English, the short-term commercial lease is a radical departure from existing forms, providing a new option for businesses wishing to occupy commercial property for a relatively short period. The aim is to take time, cost and hassle out of the process. The Short-Term Commercial Lease is endorsed by the CBI, FSB, PMA and ISVA.

Other documents will follow, catering for a range of business needs within the commercial property and construction sectors. In every case, the BPF will maintain its commitment to helping its members sustain and expand their businesses in a spirit of partnership with occupiers.

To obtain a copy of the lease, please contact Sweet & Maxwell on 0171 449 1111.

The BPF Short-Term Commercial Lease is reproduced by kind permission of the copyright holder and the publisher.

Published by Sweet & Maxwell Limited
©1999 British Property Federation

BRITISH PROPERTY FEDERATION

SHORT-TERM COMMERCIAL LEASE

IMPORTANT NOTICE

By entering into this lease the parties are undertaking legally binding obligations and should take legal advice before so doing.

It is important that tenants understand that the short-term commercial lease has been designed for property being offered for a relatively short period of occupation. The lease (and the related agreement for lease) provide for the letting to be granted **without security of tenure.** This means that, when the lease expires, the tenant will **not** have the legal right he would normally have under the Landlord and Tenant Act 1954 to apply to the court for a new tenancy. The removal of this right does not stop the landlord and tenant agreeing to a new lease at the end of the tenancy, but this can only occur if **both** the landlord and the tenant so wish.

Tenants wanting to guarantee that they can remain in the same business premises once the initial lease has expired should consult their professional advisers about seeking other premises where such terms are on offer. In such cases, the terms and conditions in the lease are likely to be substantially different from those in the BPF short-term commercial lease, particularly with regard to the nature and extent of the obligations placed on the tenant.

The BPF short-term commercial lease, and related agreement for lease, have been prepared with the overriding objective of offering a better service to business tenants. A wide-ranging consultation exercise was undertaken before the final versions of these documents were published, and many of those consulted have offered formal statements of support. The names of supporting organisations are set out on the cover. The BPF is confident that the use of this straightforward documentation will do much to enhance the relationship between landlords and tenants.

Landlords and tenants must remember that while the short-term commercial lease has been published as a standard form, it contains clauses which can be amended, or deleted, following amicable discussion between the parties.

Both landlords and tenants are strongly advised, in addition to obtaining legal advice, to consult the pan-industry document *Commercial Property Leases in England and Wales: Code of Practice* (RICS Business Services, 1995) before signing this document.

BRITISH PROPERTY FEDERATION

SHORT-TERM COMMERCIAL LEASE

MAIN TERMS AND DEFINITIONS

1. The Landlord is
   of

2. The Tenant is
   of

3. The Premises are
   [and are shown edged red on the attached plan].

4. The Term of this lease begins [immediately] [on   1999/20   ]
   and ends on   1999/20

5. The Rent is £   per year (exclusive of Value Added Tax) and is
   payable in advance by equal [monthly payments on the   day of each
   month] [quarterly payments on every 25 March, 24 June, 29 September
   and 25 December]

6. The Rent begins to be payable [immediately] [on
   1999/20   and the first payment shall be made on [that date]
   [1999/20   ].

[7. The Tenant has paid a Deposit of £   to the Landlord which the
   Landlord will place in a bank deposit account (whether or not containing
   other money) on which a reasonable rate of interest is payable. The
   Landlord will repay the Deposit to the Tenant with accrued interest once
   the Tenant has vacated the Premises at the end of the Term (however it
   ends), but less deductions properly made by the Landlord to cover any
   unpaid Rent and Value Added Tax and the actual or anticipated cost of
   remedying any breaches of the Tenant's Obligations under this Lease.]

8. The Permitted Use of the Premises is as

9. The Hours of Use are [at all times on all days] [from   am to
   pm on Mondays to Fridays, from   am to   pm on Saturdays]
   [and Sundays] [but not on [Sundays or] public holidays].

LETTING AND RIGHTS

10. The Landlord lets the Premises to the Tenant at the Rent for the Term.

11. *(Delete anything in clause 11 which does not apply)*

11.1 [The Premises form only part of a Building. They do not include any part of the main structure, foundations, roof or exterior of that Building but they do include window frames and glass, doors and door frames, raised floors and suspended ceilings and the voids above and below them, light fittings and other landlord's fixtures and fittings;]

11.2 [The Tenant is granted the shared use, [but only during the Hours of Use,] of the following Common Parts:

entrances	estate roads
hallways	car park
passages	delivery areas
staircases	yards
toilets	lifts

but must use them in a reasonable and proper manner in accordance with any regulations imposed from time to time by the Landlord;]

11.3 [The Tenant is granted the non-exclusive use of Service Media (meaning any ducts flues gutters pipes drains sewers cables conduits wires or other media for conducting water soil gas electricity and telecommunications) which serve the Premises and which may serve other premises, but must use them in a reasonable and proper manner in accordance with any regulations imposed from time to time by the Landlord;]

11.4 [The Landlord reserves the right to alter or close any Common Parts subject to providing (except in emergencies) reasonably suitable alternative amenities, and reserves the right to use (and repair, alter or renew) any Service Media in the Premises which serve other premises.]

11.5 The Landlord also reserves the right to enter the Premises for the purposes and on the terms set out elsewhere in this Lease. The right of entry will be exercised only following reasonable notice, except in the case of an emergency.

LANDLORD'S OBLIGATIONS

12. The Landlord's Obligations to be observed throughout the Term are:

12.1 As long as the Tenant pays the Rent and complies with the Tenant's Obligations, the Landlord will give exclusive possession of the Premises to the Tenant during the Term without interference by the Landlord or any superior landlord or any person deriving title under or in trust for either of them;

12.2 The Landlord will use reasonable endeavours to provide the following Landlord's Services:

(1) keeping the Premises in tenantable condition;

(delete from or add to the following as applicable)

(2) keeping in tenantable condition the Common Parts [and the structure of the building of which the Premises form part];

(3) keeping Service Media in working order;

(4) providing during the Hours of Use :

hot water to basins in the Premises

hot water to basins in Common Parts

heating of the Premises

heating of Common Parts

lighting of Common Parts

lift service in Common Parts

caretaking/porterage

but the Landlord is not obliged to —

(a) remedy damage caused by the Tenant, or

(b) remedy fair wear and tear, or

(c) put the Premises or any Common Parts or any Service Media into better condition than at the date of this Lease [as described or shown in the attached Schedule of Condition]

and the Landlord is not responsible for interruptions in any of the Landlord's Services due to matters beyond the Landlord's control.

TENANT'S OBLIGATIONS

13. The Tenant's Obligations to be observed throughout the Term are:

13.1 the Tenant will pay the Rent immediately it falls due without any deduction or set off and (if required) by bank standing order or credit transfer to the Landlord's bank account;

13.2 the Tenant will pay any value added tax chargeable on the Rent and any other sums payable under this Lease, at the same time as the sum on which it is charged;

13.3 the Tenant will pay interest on any Rent or other sum payable under this Lease which is overdue for 7 days after its due date, calculated (both before and after any court judgment) at 4% per year above the Bank of England base rate for the period from the due date until payment;

13.4 the Tenant will pay all charges for all water, gas, electricity, telephone and similar services consumed on the Premises, and will pay a fair proportion of any which relate to both the Premises and other premises;

13.5 the Tenant will take reasonable care of the Premises and will not damage them, but normal fair wear and tear is permitted;

13.6 the Tenant will comply with all legislation applicable to the Tenant's use of the Premises; the Tenant will not do anything which may result in a statutory requirement arising for work to be carried out on the Premises or any other premises of the Landlord;

13.7 the Tenant will immediately give the Landlord a copy of any notice relating to the Premises or its use which the Tenant receives and will also notify the Landlord of any damage to or want of repair in the Premises or the building of which they form part, as soon as reasonably possible after becoming aware of it;

13.8 the Tenant will not make any alteration or addition to the Premises (including displaying any signs, posters, advertisements, etc.) inside or outside, and will remove any unauthorised alterations or additions on demand;

BUSINESS RATES   14.   It is one of the Landlord's Obligations that the Landlord pay the business rates in respect of the Premises

It is one of the Tenant's Obligations that the Tenant pay the business rates in respect of the Premises.

(Delete which of the above does not apply)

BREACH OF TENANT'S OBLIGATIONS   15.   If the Landlord serves on the Tenant a written notice specifying anything required to remedy a breach of the Tenant's Obligations under this Lease —

15.1   the Tenant will comply with the notice within one month (or immediately in emergency);

15.2   if the Tenant fails to do so, the Landlord has the right to enter the Premises and remedy the breach and the Tenant will pay to the Landlord on demand, as a debt, all costs and expenses so incurred by the Landlord.

TENANT'S GOODS AT THE PREMISES   16.   If the Tenant leaves any goods in the Premises at the end of the Term (however it ends), the Tenant authorises the Landlord to sell those goods on behalf of the Tenant. The Landlord shall account to the Tenant for the proceeds less the Landlord's reasonable expenses.

CONSEQUENCES OF DAMAGE OR DESTRUCTION   17.   If the whole or part of the Premises becomes inaccessible or unfit for use due to damage or destruction (other than as a result of anything the Tenant does or fails to do):

17.1   the whole or an appropriate proportion (having regard to the nature and extent of the destruction or damage) of the Rent and other payments under this Lease shall cease to be payable until the Premises are fully accessible and fit for use; and

17.2   if the damage or destruction affects the whole or a substantial part of the Premises and it is likely to take more than three months to make the Premises again fully accessible and fit for use, either the Landlord or the Tenant may terminate this Lease by giving written notice to the other, in which event this Lease will immediately end and the Landlord need not carry out any repairs or reinstatement.

FORFEITURE   18.   The Landlord may forfeit this Lease by re-entering the Premises (or part of them as if entering the whole) if:

(a)   any Rent or other sums are overdue for 14 days or more (whether or not demanded), or

(b)   if any of the Tenant's Obligations under this Lease are not performed or observed, or

(c)   if the Tenant (being an individual) becomes bankrupt, or

(d)   if the Tenant (being a company) enters into liquidation whether voluntary or compulsory (unless for the purpose of reconstruction or amalgamation) or has a receiver or administrative receiver appointed over any of its assets or is the subject of a petition for the appointment of an administrator, or

(e)   if the Tenant enters into an arrangement or composition with creditors, and on re-entry the Term will end but the Landlord will retain any accrued rights in respect of breaches of the Tenant's Obligations.

GENERAL PROVISIONS

19. Notices relating to this Lease or to the Premises may be served in accordance with Law of Property Act 1925 section 196.

20. The Landlord and the Tenant agree that Landlord and Tenant Act 1954 sections 24 to 28 do not apply. This provision is authorised by an order of the   County Court dated 1999/20

21. It is also agreed that:

21.1 the Tenant will not have any rights over any property of the Landlord or the benefit of any obligations on the part of the Landlord, except as set out in this Lease;

21.2 where a party to this Lease comprises two or more persons, they are responsible for all their obligations both jointly and individually;

21.3 where this Lease obliges the Tenant not to do something, the Tenant is also obliged not to permit it to be done by any person under the Tenant's control;

21.4 headings are given in this Lease for convenience only and do not affect the meaning of the text.

[BREAK CLAUSE

22. Either the Landlord or the Tenant may give to the other not less than   months'/weeks'/days' written notice to end the Term on the   1999/20   [or on any later date]. Ending the Term will not release the parties from their accrued liabilities down to that date.]

[CERTIFICATE FOR STAMPING

23. There is no written agreement for the grant of this lease.]

SIGNED   ....
(Landlord/Tenant)

DATE OF THIS LEASE: ....1999/20.....